QUILTS

Masterworks from the American Folk Art Museum

QUILTS

Masterworks from the American Folk Art Museum

Elizabeth V. Warren

with a preface by **Maria Ann Conelli**

a foreword by **Martha Stewart**

and an introduction by **Stacy C. Hollander**

RIZZOLI
NEW YORK

New York · Paris · London · Milan

in association with the **American Folk Art Museum, New York**

Published by Rizzoli International Publications, Inc.

300 Park Avenue South

New York, NY 10010

www.rizzoliusa.com

in association with

American Folk Art Museum, New York

www.folkartmuseum.org

2010 2011 2012 2013 / 10 9 8 7 6 5 4 3 2 1

Edited by Mareike Grover and Tanya Heinrich

Copyedited by Victoria Brown

Designed by Laura Lindgren

Endpapers: detail of page 135; page 1: detail of page 73; pages 2–3: detail of page 183;
pages 4–5: detail of page 78; pages 6–7: detail of page 213; page 8: see page 229;
page 9: detail of page 54; pages 10–11: detail of page 63; page 12: detail of page 219;
page 14: detail of page 238; page 16: detail of page 139

ISBN: 978-08478-3373-3

Printed in China

Library of Congress Control Number: 2010922523

Contents

Preface

Maria Ann Conelli

The American Folk Art Museum has been collecting and showcasing quilts since its inception in the early 1960s. By the mid-1990s, the museum's holdings of American quilts had grown to merit the publication of a comprehensive collection catalog. Written by Elizabeth V. Warren and Sharon L. Eisenstat, *Glorious American Quilts* documented almost four hundred bedcovers from the late eighteenth century to the present. In the ensuing fourteen years, the collection has expanded to encompass approximately five hundred quilts, and the museum is proud to present about two hundred of these stunning textiles in the pages of this book.

The museum's unparalleled collection of quilts would not be what it is today without the accomplishments of former directors Robert Bishop and Gerard C. Wertkin and several of its trustees and patrons. It was their collective passion and enthusiasm that inspired countless individuals and organizations to bestow upon the museum hundreds of bedcovers of singular beauty.

I would like to thank Elizabeth V. Warren for her decades-long commitment to the museum's documentation, study, preservation, and exhibition of quilts. A respected scholar in this field, Liz is also a valued member of the museum's board of trustees. Without her tireless dedication, this beautiful volume could not have been published.

Stacy C. Hollander, the museum's senior curator and director of exhibitions, who has organized a vast number of inspired quilt exhibitions and is an integral part of this publication, deserves my sincere gratitude. Her comprehensive knowledge of the museum's quilt collection assured that the finest examples of each genre were selected and illustrated.

I would like to extend my thanks to the staff of the American Folk Art Museum who devoted countless hours to the making of this book: Linda Dunne, deputy director, for overseeing the project; Ann-Marie Reilly, chief registrar and director of exhibition production, and Courtney Wagner, manager of photographic services, for facilitating the photography; and Tanya Heinrich, director of publications, and Mareike Grover, managing editor, whose organizational talents and editorial precision are transformational.

At Rizzoli International Publications, my sincere thanks go to publisher Charles Miers, who conceived of the book, as well as to senior editor Christopher Steighner and assistant editor Jono Jarrett. Thanks also go to designer Laura Lindgren, who turned hundreds of manuscript pages and images into this gorgeous book.

Last but not least, I would like to thank Martha Stewart for her participation, for her continued support of the museum, and for her love of the field.

The most rewarding part of any museum director's job is the opportunity to work with talented and committed individuals, to experience the joy of seeing a publication such as this come to fruition, and to share exceptional works of art with the public.

FOREWORD

Martha Stewart

This is an impressive book highlighting the most notable quilts found in a most notable quilt collection located in the holdings of the American Folk Art Museum.

Quilts have an interesting history, amazing stories about their creation abound, and the techniques used by their makers vary extensively from whole-cloth quilts fabricated from large pieces of fabric to Log Cabin quilts pieced from hundreds of small bits of cloth. This book covers eleven categories of quilts, and the reader is constantly surprised, page after page, by the ingenuity, the stitchery, the handiwork, the craftsmanship, the variety, the materials, and the artistry found in every quilt. The vision required of each maker, or group of makers, is mind-boggling when one considers the *Tree of Life Whitework Quilt* (page 41), the *Sunburst Quilt* (page 63), the *Bird of Paradise Quilt Top* (page 111), the *Log Cabin Quilt, Barn Raising Variation* (page 156), the *Roses and Ribbons Quilt* (page 221), or the *Inside Border Child's Quilt* (page 254).

I have been looking at quilts for many, many years—at auctions, tag sales, antiques shows, and museum exhibitions. In the 1960s, after I got married, I started buying quilts that appealed to my design sensibility, quilts that actually fit into my decorating schemes in my New York apartment and my small country house in Middlefield, Massachusetts. I especially liked chintz quilts and whitework quilts; I cherished them as bedcovers, as throws over the backs of sofas and chairs, and as wall decoration. When I came across quilts that were worn, torn, or fragmented, I made use of them as table coverings for country suppers. I read about and studied quilts and their textiles, informally, in books by the collector Nina Fletcher Little; in the wonderful catalog *The Flowering of American Folk Art, 1776–1876* by Jean Lipman and Alice Winchester (which accompanied the Whitney Museum of American Art's great 1974 exhibition of the same name); and in the numerous books about quilts published by Dutton.

Eclectic accumulator that I am, I never really "collected" in any serious fashion this superb category of American folk art—but looking at the quilts pictured in this tome makes me wish I had. What nimble fingers, what imagination, what lovely combinations of coloring and patterning, and what extraordinary artisanship went into the fabrication of these works of art. A whole-cloth quilt could be astonishingly simple, emphasizing the cloth, or exceedingly complex, with complicated stitchery. The Log Cabin quilts, with infinite numbers of pieces of cloth, and variations on a theme, have mass appeal. The Amish quilts, with their geometric simplicity, are reminders to us that modern art started way before the twentieth century. The African American quilts exemplify practicality, reuse of materials, and a true sense of design, while the show quilts simply inspire and amaze.

There is a style of quilt for every taste, and every taste will discover more than a few quilts to covet and admire. Ms. Warren and the American Folk Art Museum should be proud of this book that every library should contain.

INTRODUCTION The Quilt Collection of the American Folk Art Museum

Stacy C. Hollander

During the time in which the American Folk Art Museum was formed, in the early 1960s, there was but a hint of the popular interest in quilts that was to explode in the following decade. Two significant events, the groundbreaking 1971 exhibition "Abstract Design in American Quilts," at the Whitney Museum of American Art in New York, and the American bicentennial celebrations in 1976, focused attention on quilts as art and refocused attention on arts with a historical American past. "Abstract Design in American Quilts," organized by Jonathan Holstein and Gail van der Hoof and based on their own collection, unapologetically placed quilts on museum walls as powerful works of abstract art. Implicit in this act was a recognition of the important and largely unacknowledged contribution of women to American visual arts. Perhaps not coincidentally, this was also the period that gave rise to the women's movement and the ensuing field of women's studies. Quilts, physically and visually monumental testaments to the ongoing creativity and participation of women in American life, became emblematic of the silent majority: vital and beautiful, powerful and skilled, individual and diverse—and hidden in plain sight.

The American Folk Art Museum was in the vanguard of the renewed appreciation of quilts that was to flower in the 1970s and that continues unabated into the present. From its beginnings, the museum's mission was grounded in the consideration of the artistic merits of the works it collected and exhibited. Quilts were occasionally on view during the institution's first decade, but it was not until 1972 that an exhibition entirely devoted to textile arts was presented: "The Fabric of the State" examined textiles, including quilts, made specifically in New York. Coincidentally, this was the same year the museum first accepted a quilt into its holdings, a late-nineteenth-century Crazy quilt. Since then, the museum's quilt collection has grown to approximately five hundred important examples dating from the late eighteenth century to the present, a considerable accomplishment in that it was formed almost entirely through gifts. As a result, the collection does not claim to be encyclopedic in scope (though it is nearly so) and necessarily reflects the taste and collecting trends of the many generous donors who have benefitted the museum throughout its institutional life. It is the museum's great fortune that the majority of the quilts were collected at a time when they were still undervalued in the art world and extraordinary examples were available for acquisition to those with a refined eye. The collection today is particularly strong in Amish quilts, whiteworks, Victorian show quilts, Double Wedding Ring quilts, and twentieth-century Revival quilts; it also boasts singular examples of narrative, stenciled, pieced, and appliquéd quilts and bedcovers. Though some quilts descended within a family and came to the museum with their histories intact, most have become divorced from their particular circumstances over time; only fragments of their stories can be pieced together, revealed through a study of the fabrics, compositions, and techniques. One of the newest additions to the collection is also one of the most recently stitched: *Kaleidoscopic XVI: More Is More* (page 315) is a gift of the artist, Paula Nadelstern, the first living quilt artist to receive a monographic exhibition at the museum, in 2009.

The American Folk Art Museum achieved status as a major center of American quilt artistry under the leadership of Robert Bishop, a gifted director (1977–1991) with a profound belief in the deserved place of quilts in the art canon. Bishop's ambitions for the institution immediately broadened the scope of interest with the 1979 exhibition "Hawaiian Quilts: Treasures of an Island Folk Art" and culminated in the establishment of the Great American Quilt Festival. The core of the museum's quilt collection was formed through Bishop's energetic cultivation of gifts from a variety of sources. Board member Cyril Irwin Nelson, an eminent editor at Dutton and innovator of the *Quilt Engagement Calendar*, was especially instrumental in this effort through gifts of masterpieces from his own collection, such as the *Harlequin Medallion Quilt* (page 26) and the *Pieties Quilt* (page 124). Each year until Nelson's death in 2005, the museum could depend on additional breathtaking gifts from his collection, a tradition that has since been continued by Nelson's family. In 1979, the museum's board of trustees purchased the enduringly popular *Bird of Paradise Quilt Top* (page 111) that had graced the cover of the publication accompanying the Whitney's seminal 1974 exhibition "The Flowering of American Folk Art, 1776–1876." Also in 1979, the museum received a gift of two spectacular nineteenth-century quilts made by members of a well-known Philadelphia Quaker family, the Saverys (pages 63 and 67). A year later, the renowned collector and dealer David Pottinger single-handedly made the museum a major repository of Amish quilts through his gift of almost one hundred examples from Midwestern Amish communities. This acquisition was complemented in 1984 by a group of exquisite Amish quilts from Lancaster and Mifflin Counties in Pennsylvania, generously donated by William and Dede Wigton. More recently, the museum's holdings of Amish and Mennonite quilts have been augmented by a gift of almost a dozen quilts from Alan and Nina Weinstein, as well as by several gifts from individual donors. By 1985, the collection had come full circle with the addition of a wonderful group of late-nineteenth-century Crazy and show quilts gifted by Margaret Cavigga.

The Great American Quilt Festival, instituted by Robert Bishop in 1986, was one of the nation's first and largest events to celebrate the art of quiltmaking and offered multiple exhibitions, educational programming, hands-on workshops and classes, and showcases by commercial vendors. Occupying a large pier on New York's waterfront, the first Festival was themed around the one hundredth anniversary of the Statue of Liberty. Competitions based on this idea resulted in some of the museum's first acquisitions of contemporary pictorial quilts and set a high standard for the Festivals that followed. Under the museum's aegis, the Festival brought hundreds of thousands of visitors interested in quiltmaking as both a historical and a living art to New York. It also raised funds for the museum to purchase quilts for the collection. In 1991, art historian Dr. Maude Southwell Wahlman was invited to identify quilts made by African American quiltmakers from the rural South for purchase with funds provided by a grant from the National Endowment for the Arts and matched through proceeds from the Great American Quilt Festival 3. A collection of twenty contemporary quilts was assembled, made primarily in Georgia, Alabama, and Mississippi and including examples from Gee's Bend.

In 1985, the museum conceived another major initiative with the organization of the New York Quilt Project. Under the direction of Folk Art Institute registrar Phyllis A. Tepper, this mammoth undertaking recorded six thousand quilts in forty-five quilt-documentation days held throughout the state. Highlights were featured in the 1992 book *New York Beauties: Quilts from the Empire State* and exhibited at the museum in 1994. The beautiful *Star of Bethlehem Quilt* (page 181) was discovered during the course of this project and subsequently purchased by the museum. One of the most dazzling and historically significant show quilts in the collection today, it descended within the family of Jeremiah Sullivan Black, attorney general of the United States from 1857 to 1860, and exemplifies the vogue for luxurious and delicate silk show quilts that was to characterize the latter part of the nineteenth century.

In 1996, *Glorious American Quilts* was published. Written by Elizabeth V. Warren and Sharon L. Eisenstat, it was the first complete catalog of the museum's quilt collection and counted 398 quilts in its holdings at the time. In the years since, and under the stewardship of Gerard C. Wertkin, director of the museum from 1991 to 2004, and the current executive director, Maria Ann Conelli, about one hundred prominent quilts have entered the collection, very few of which have, up until now, been written about or reproduced in print. Notable among these acquisitions is the c. 1831 *Stenciled Quilt* from Massachusetts (page 39), a beautiful and pristine example of the technique and an unexpected gift from In the Beginning Quilts, Inc., Seattle. A true surprise was the *Surprise Quilt Presented to Mary A. Grow* (page 69), a mid-nineteenth-century friendship quilt from Michigan that had descended in the family of Eleanor Stoddard Seibold and was donated in her memory by her husband, Fred Seibold. A deeply moving album quilt, rich in mourning symbolism and made as a presentation for William A. Sargent (page 81), was one of the last gifts made by Cyril Irwin Nelson before his death. More recently, the museum has received a splendid *Baltimore-Style Album Quilt Top* (page 73) from the corporate collections of Altria Group, Inc., and a rare and precious quilt with a center block by the renowned colonial printer John Hewson (page 57) that was bestowed by Jerry and Susan Lauren.

Strategically located in the heart of the exciting and culturally competitive environment of New York City, the American Folk Art Museum has played an unparalleled role in advocating for quilts and broadening the discourse of this form within the larger picture of American art. Quilts appeared on no fewer than twenty-two covers of the museum's *Folk Art* magazine, and its pages related more than fifty articles devoted to quilt artistry and history. Exhibitions such as "White on White (and a little gray)" (2006), "Ancestry and Innovation: African American Art from the Collection" (2005), "Talking Quilts" (2004), and "Beyond the Square: Color and Design in Amish Quilts" (1999), among many others, have expanded the arenas in which quilts have been considered. Notwithstanding the American Folk Art Museum's spirited championship, and as these pages gloriously demonstrate, the quilts and the generations of voices behind them speak eloquently for themselves.

THE WHOLE-CLOTH QUILT

The term *whole-cloth quilt* refers to bedcovers made of large pieces of either solid-colored wool (pages 22–29) or silk, printed chintz or copperplate-printed cotton or linen (pages 30–33), stenciled cotton (pages 34–39), or one of the various forms of embroidered cotton or linen known as "whitework" (pages 40–47). These are among the earliest forms of American bedcovers and, without firm provenance, are often difficult to distinguish from similar examples made in England, where the American quiltmaking tradition originated.

Technically, the quilts that are called whole-cloth are not made of one piece of fabric. Eighteenth- and early-nineteenth-century looms were too narrow to permit production of fabric that was large enough to cover the entire surface of the beds of the period, which were often piled high with feather mattresses or straw ticks. Consequently, a number of pieces of fabric, occasionally of different colors or patterns, would be seamed together to form the quilt top, which was then usually quilted with motifs that covered the entire surface. The beautiful *Indigo Calimanco Quilt* (page 23), for example, displays

particularly well executed examples of fruit and floral designs that may have been derived from Jacobean crewel embroidery.

Whole-cloth wool quilts, for many years mistakenly referred to as "linsey-woolseys," were often made of a professionally manufactured glazed fabric known as "calimanco." In the eighteenth century, this type of fabric was more common for clothing, especially quilted petticoats, and sometimes the fabric used for the bedcovers was rescued from worn petticoats. For example, it is likely that the bright calimanco pieces in the *Harlequin Medallion Quilt* (page 26) were salvaged from other uses.

Cotton and linen whole-cloth quilts from the late eighteenth and early nineteenth centuries are among the rarest American bedcovers and provide a wonderful opportunity for textile historians to study large lengths of fabric. The chintz whole-cloth quilts (pages 30 and 31) are both made of glazed cotton fabrics printed in designs and colors popular at the beginning of the nineteenth century and probably originally manufactured for home furnishings such as drapery and upholstery. The *Copperplate-Printed Whole-Cloth Quilt* (page 33) is made from a linen-and-cotton fabric identified as Bamboo Trails, a pattern produced by the well-known English textile manufactory at Bromley Hall, near London.

Stenciled bedcovers are also relatively rare (approximately sixty have been identified) and were made primarily in New England and New York State. Stencil decoration on fabric is closely related to the early-nineteenth-century vogue for paint-decorated walls and furniture, as well as the theorems, or stenciled still-life and landscape paintings executed by young ladies on velvet, silk, or paper. About half of the known stenciled bedcovers were neither backed nor quilted and are composed of a single layer of cotton decorated with paint, such as the *Pots of Flowers Stenciled Spread* (page 35)

and the *Block-Work Stenciled Spread* (page 37). When stenciled bedcovers are quilted (see page 39), they most frequently combine stenciled and painted blocks with chintz blocks.

The fashion for all-white textiles at the end of the eighteenth and the beginning of the nineteenth centuries has been related to the popularity of neoclassicism in furnishing and clothing styles, as well as to the increased availability of both cotton fabric and the cotton thread necessary for the complex quilting and embroidery that is generally a hallmark of whitework bedcovers. The examples of whitework shown here illustrate a number of the techniques employed by quiltmakers for this most elegant style: elaborate stuffing and cording (page 41), candlewick embroidery (pages 42 and 45), and precise and delicate stitching.

Indigo Calimanco Quilt

Artist unidentified

Probably New England

1800–1820

The Whole-Cloth Quilt

Harlequin Medallion Quilt

Artist unidentified

New England

1800–1820

Center Star Quilt

Artist unidentified

New England

1815–1825

The Whole-Cloth Quilt

Pieced Quilt

Artist unidentified

New England

1810–1820

Pieced Quilt

Artist unidentified

Probably New England

1820–1840

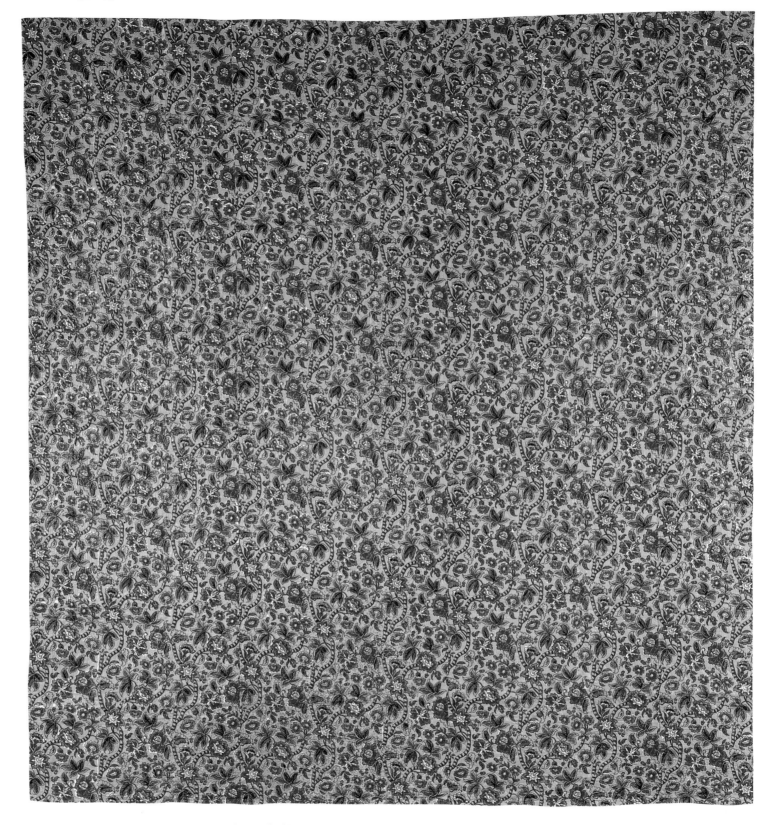

Chintz Whole-Cloth Quilt

Artist unidentified

Probably United States

1810–1820

Chintz Whole-Cloth Quilt

Artist unidentified

Probably United States

1830–1840

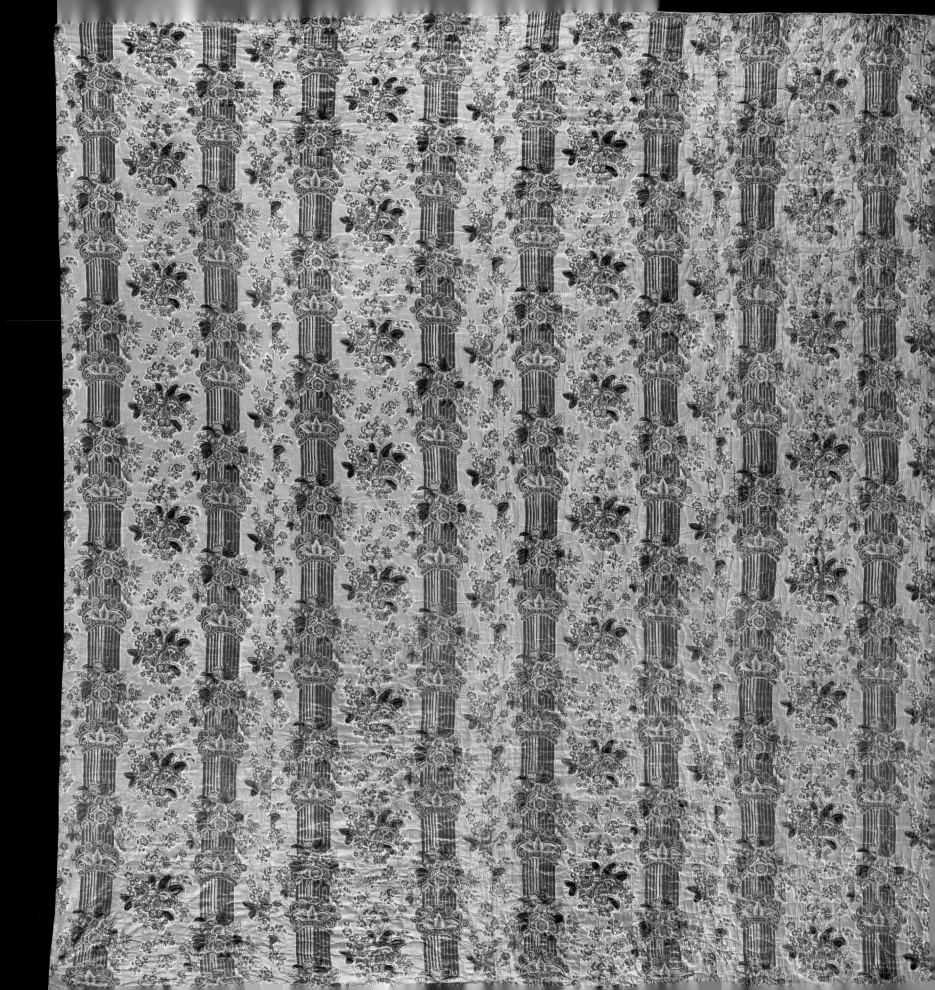

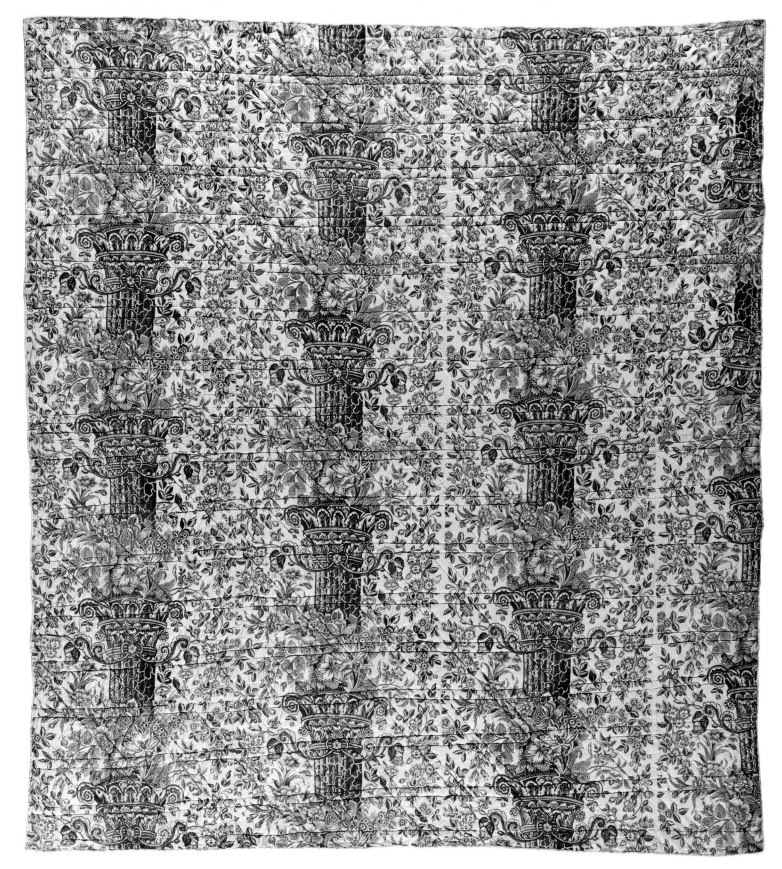

Pillar-Print Whole-Cloth Quilt

Artist unidentified

United States

1825–1835

Copperplate-Printed Whole-Cloth Quilt

Artist unidentified

Probably England

1785–1790

Block-Work Stenciled Spread

Possibly Sara Massey (dates unknown)

Possibly Watertown, New York

1825–1840

Stenciled Quilt

Olivia Dunham Barnes (1807–1887)

Conway, Massachusetts

1825–1835

Candlewick Spread

Maria Clark (1799–1871)

Coventry, Connecticut

1825–1840

Cornucopia and Dots Whitework Quilt

Artist unidentified

United States

1800–1820

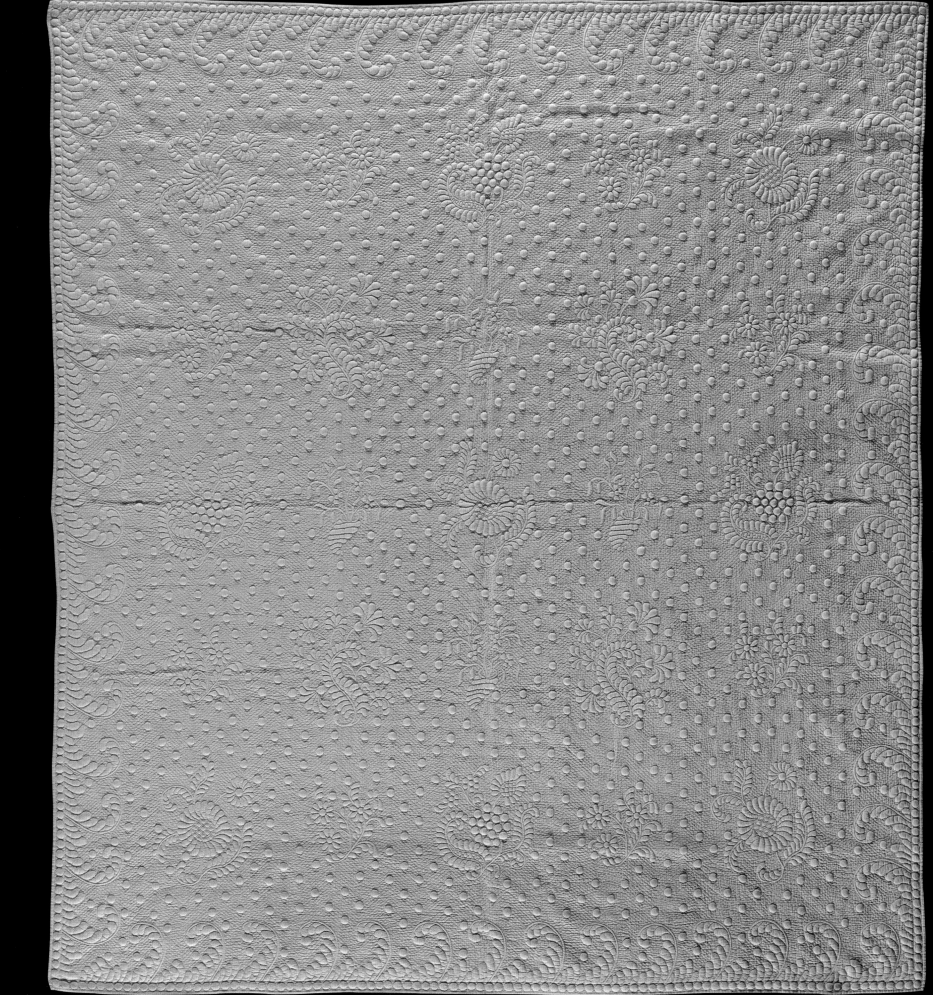

THE CHINTZ QUILT

The chintz quilt tradition includes bedcovers made of appliquéd cut-out pieces of fabric (pages 50–51) and those composed of pieced scraps (pages 52 and 56–63), as well as textiles that combine the two techniques (pages 53–55). These styles were popular in America from the late eighteenth to the middle of the nineteenth centuries and are considered among the earliest varieties of patchwork quilts.

The term *chintz* is derived from the Hindu word *chitta*, meaning "spotted cloth." The first examples of this cloth were brought to England from India by sixteenth-century traders. Over the years, the word has come to refer to a large-scale print, usually finished with a glaze, that is suitable for furnishings such as drapery and upholstery.

Cut-out chintz quilts are characterized by printed designs taken from one piece of fabric and appliquéd onto another. In the first half of the nineteenth century, particularly between 1820 and 1840, a number of fabrics were printed specifically for use in quilts. Bold central motifs, borders, and smaller designs would be combined in a single fabric that could be cut out and appliquéd onto a quilt top of the maker's own planning. The *Cut-out Chintz Quilt with Sawtooth Border* (page 50) and the *Cut-out Chintz Quilt with Chintz Border* (page 51) were made using these fabrics.

Probably the oldest chintz quilt in the museum's collection, the *Hewson-Center Quilt with Multiple Borders* (page 57), combines a printed chintz center with a series of pieced borders that employ a variety of fabrics, including chintz. The center block of this quilt (possibly printed as early as 1790) is typical of those produced by the English immigrant textile printer and manufacturer John Hewson (1744–1821). To date, twenty-eight textiles displaying Hewson's printing have been documented; in almost all of them, a vase-and-flowers panel as the one in the museum's quilt takes center position. In some cases, the motifs are cut out and appliquéd in an individual design, while on other examples, including this quilt, the panel is used exactly as printed.

While most of the quilts in this section have been constructed using the traditional "running-stitch" or

"American" method of piecing, two of the museum's chintz quilts were pieced using what is known as the "whipstitch," "paper-template," or "English patchwork" technique. This time-consuming method was employed most often for quilts made in all-over mosaic-type patterns and involved paper templates to line each piece. In January 1835, *Godey's Lady's Book* printed instructions for one of the most popular patterns to utilize the template method: Hexagon (also called Six-sided or Honeycomb) Patchwork, exemplified here by the *Honeycomb Quilt Top* (page 61).

Diamond Patchwork, seen in the *Sunburst Quilt* (page 63), was also commonly executed using the paper-template method. Approximately 2,900 diamonds were joined to form this large and historically important quilt. Six quilts, including the *Friendship Star Quilt* (page 67), are known to be associated with the probable maker of the *Sunburst Quilt*, Rebecca Scattergood Savery, a member of a prominent Philadelphia Quaker family in the late eighteenth and nineteenth centuries.

Cut-out Chintz Quilt with Sawtooth Border

Artist unidentified

Pennsylvania

1835–1850

Cut-out Chintz Quilt with Chintz Border

Artist unidentified

Possibly New England

1835–1850

The Chintz Quilt

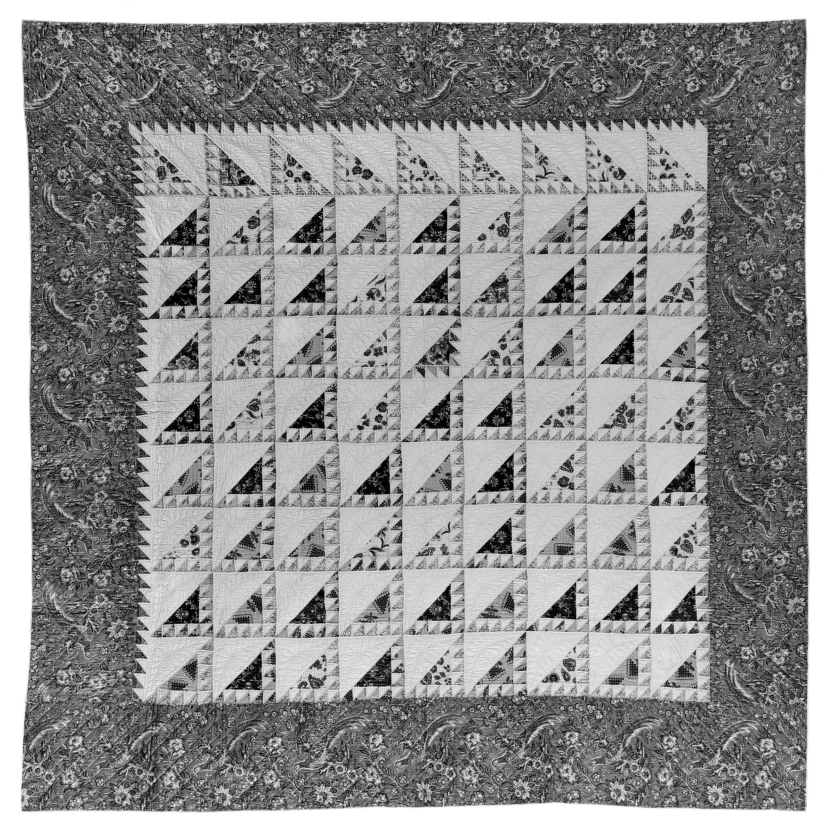

Lady of the Lake Quilt

Artist unidentified, initialed "E.M."

United States

Dated 1837

Center Medallion and Flying Geese Quilt

Artist unidentified

New England

1825–1835

Variable Stars Quilt

Artist unidentified

New England

1825–1840

Carpenter's Wheel Quilt

Artist unidentified

Pennsylvania

1835–1845

Hewson-Center Quilt with Multiple Borders

Artist unidentified; center block printed by John Hewson (1744–1821)

United States

1790–1810

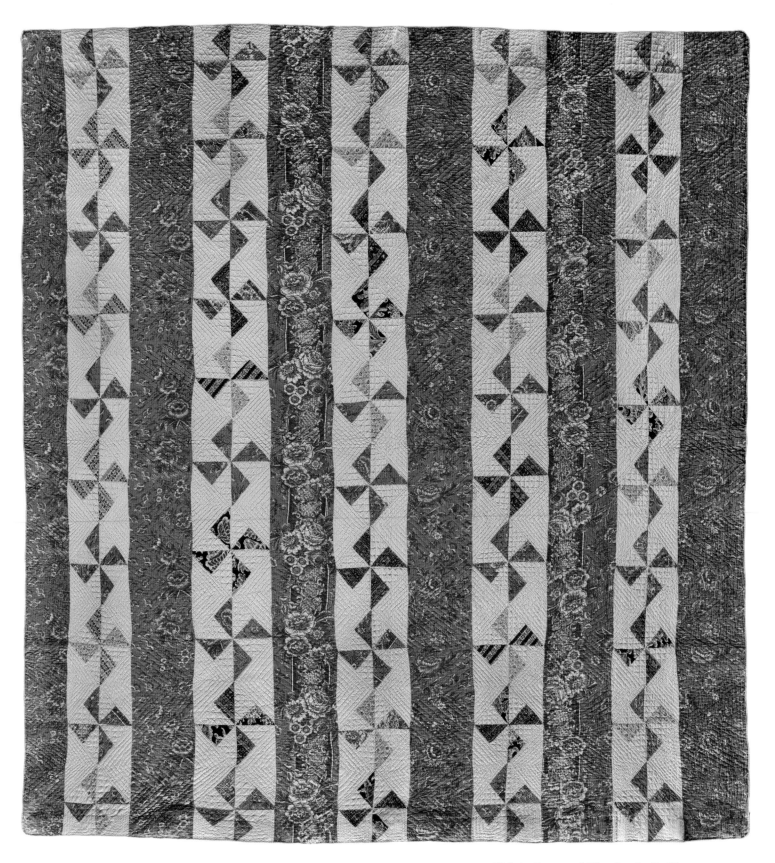

Nine-Patch Variation Quilt

Artist unidentified

Probably New England

1830–1840

Chintz Bars and Pinwheels Quilt

Artist unidentified

United States

1830–1850

Honeycomb Quilt Top

Artist unidentified

United States or England

1835–1845

The Chintz Quilt

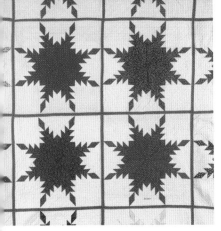

THE SIGNATURE QUILT

The bedcovers illustrated in this section represent a fashion for signed quilt blocks that started in the early 1840s, reached its peak by midcentury, and began to fade in the late 1850s. The custom experienced a revival, albeit with some changes, in the late nineteenth and early twentieth centuries.

Most signature quilts belong to a tradition of group projects: the blocks were made by, paid for, and/ or signed by different people, and the squares were then assembled by either a single quiltmaker or a group working together. The quilts also can be related to the fondness young ladies in the early nineteenth century held for collecting autographs in albums. Signature quilts were often made on the occasion of an engagement or marriage, or as a gift when a member of the community moved or retired.

Friendship quilt is the term most often used to indicate that all (or most) blocks on a signature quilt are made of the same design. The *Friendship Star Quilt* (page 67), for example, is composed of pieced six-pointed stars, each of which carries a cursive or printed signature

and a drawn or stamped design in the hexagon that forms its center. Similarly, each of the sixteen blocks of the *Surprise Quilt Presented to Mary A. Grow* (page 69) contains the name of a friend in Plymouth, Michigan, who contributed to the gift for Grow in 1856.

Quilts composed of blocks made in a number of different patterns are usually called "sampler albums." Often the blocks were sewn using a variety of techniques, including cut-out chintz appliqué, conventional appliqué, piecing, and embroidery. Probably the best-known sampler albums are those made in Baltimore between about 1845 and 1855. The museum's collection includes three distinct examples of these renowned quilts, each representative of a different style. The *Baltimore-Style Album Quilt Top* on page 70 falls into a group identified as the work of "Designer 1," a hand attributed to a woman named Mary Heidenroder Simon (1810–1893). She most likely designed and basted the distinctive blocks seen here—including the eagle with flag, the basket with book, and the cornucopia—and then sold them to the ladies of Baltimore who would finish the blocks and sew them together. The *Baltimore-Style Album Quilt Top* on page 73 is included in the group of quilts attributed to "Designer 2," although it is now believed that, since the quilts are not always as balanced and uniform in design as those in the Designer 1 group, bedcovers in this category were probably made by a group of women working together. Quilts in both the Designer 1 and Designer 2 groups have long been associated with makers who were members of the Protestant churches in Baltimore.

Another Baltimore-style album quilt in the museum's collection is the *Reiter Family Album Quilt* (page 75). For many years, this textile was in the possession of members of a family that had settled in Pennsylvania, and family history states that it was made there at the end of the nineteenth century. Research, however, has shown that the quilt shares many characteristics (including the blocks depicting an elephant and a horse and rider) with a group of distinctive quilts made by women who were members of a Hebrew congregation in Baltimore. These quilts have been dated to the same mid-nineteenth-century period as those made by the Protestant women.

In the 1880s, a distinctive style of signature quilt known as a "fund-raising quilt" became popular. While many of the album quilts made earlier may have been used as fund-raisers, there is little doubt about the purpose of the textiles in this category. For a specified payment, often a dime, quiltmakers would ink or embroider the names of donors onto the top of the quilt. The finished quilt might be given to a distinguished person in the community, or it could be auctioned or raffled to raise additional funds. Examples of these fund-raising quilts include the *Schoolhouse Quilt Top* (page 84), the *Admiral Dewey Commemorative Quilt* (page 87), and the *McKinley Community Church Signature Quilt* (page 89).

Friendship Star Quilt

Elizabeth Hooten (Cresson) Savery (dates unknown) and others

Philadelphia

Dated 1844

Surprise Quilt Presented to Mary A. Grow

Various quiltmakers

Plymouth, Michigan

Dated 1856

Baltimore-Style Album Quilt Top

Possibly Mary Heidenroder Simon (1810–1893)

Probably Baltimore

1849–1852

Baltimore-Style Album Quilt Top

Artist unidentified

Baltimore; found in Uniontown, Pennsylvania

1845–1850

Reiter Family Album Quilt

Artist unidentified, descended in the family of

Katie Friedman Reiter (1873–1942) and

Liebe Gross Friedman (dates unknown)

Probably Baltimore

1848–1850

Album Quilt

Possibly Sarah Morrell (dates unknown) and others

Pennsylvania and New Jersey

Dated 1843

 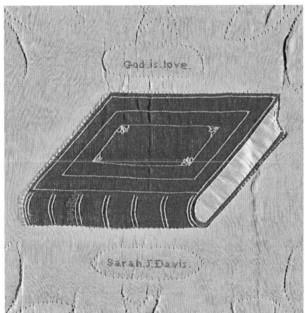 

Dunn Album Quilt

Sewing Society of the Fulton Street United Methodist Episcopal Church

Elizabethport, New Jersey

Dated 1852

Presentation Quilt for William A. Sargent

Members of the Freewill Baptist Church

Loudon, New Hampshire

Blocks made c. 1854, assembled and quilted later

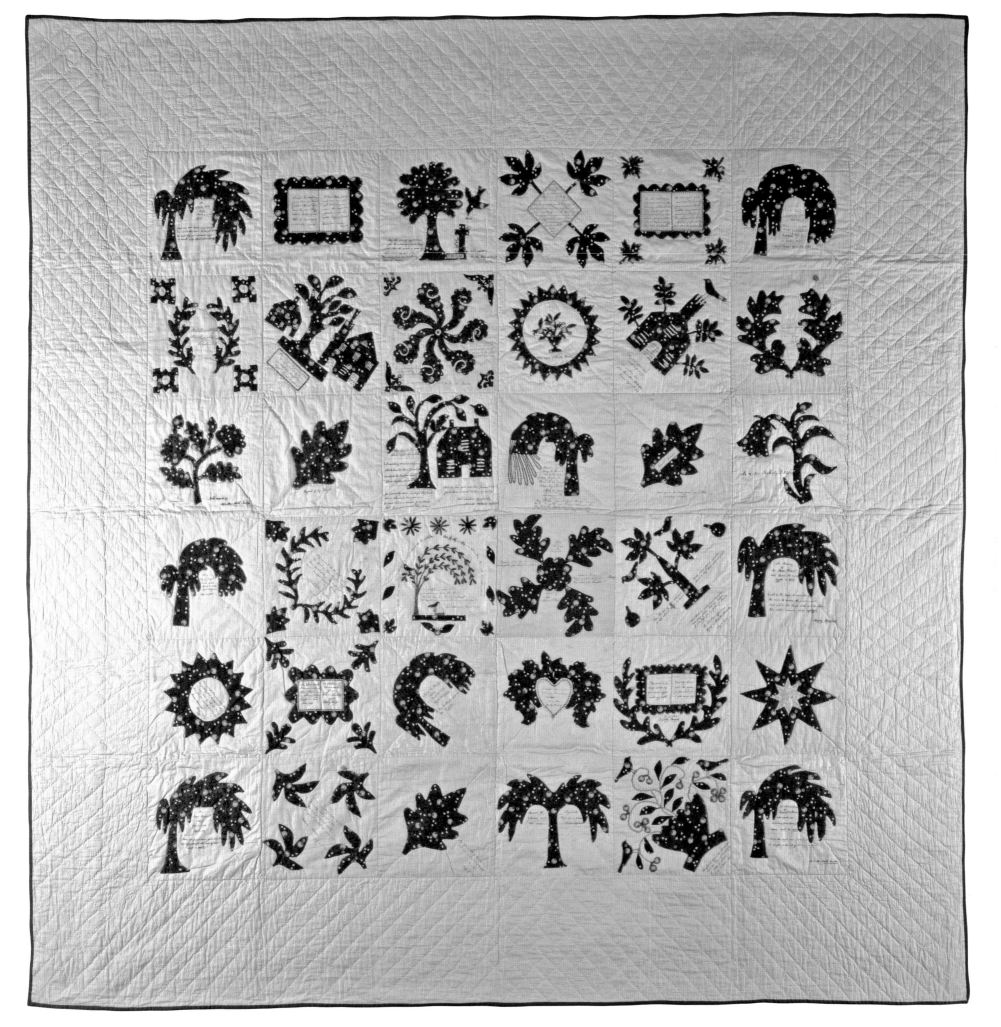

Cross River Album Quilt

Mrs. Eldad Miller (1805–1874) and others

Cross River, New York

Dated 1861

Schoolhouse Quilt Top

The Presbyterian Ladies of Oak Ridge, Missouri

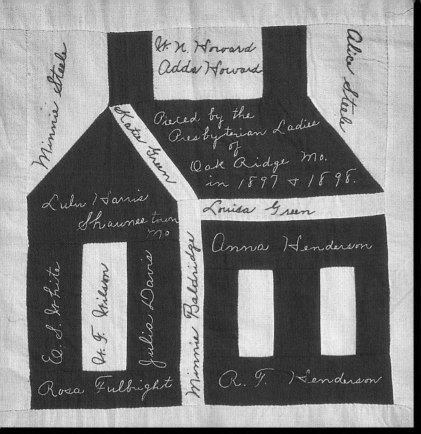
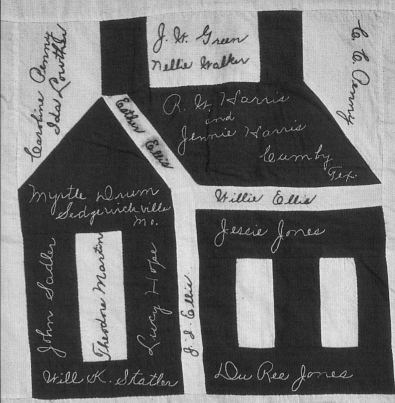
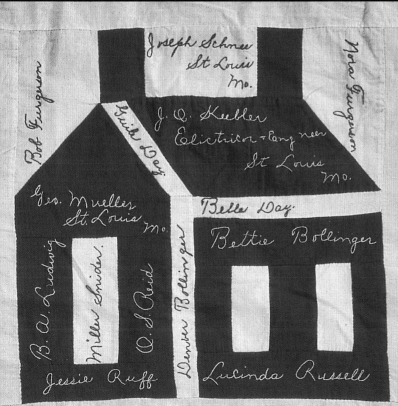
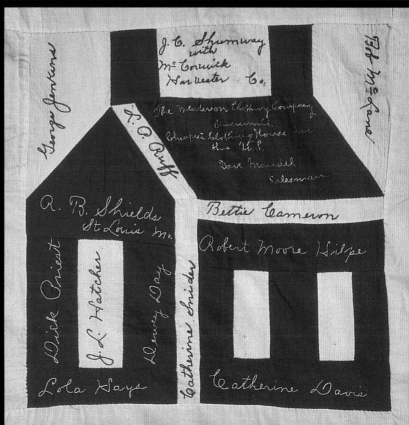

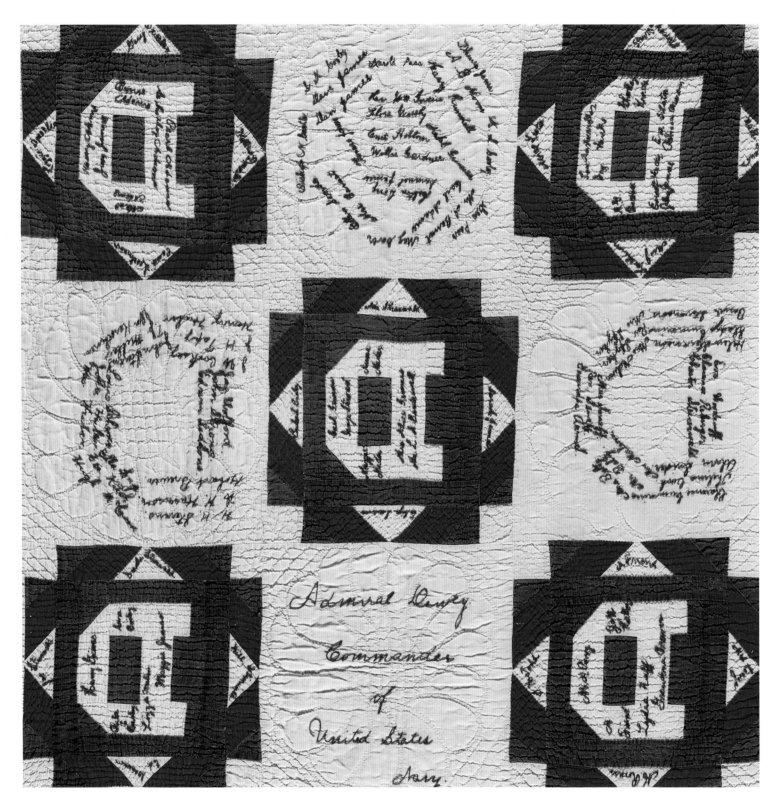

Admiral Dewey Commemorative Quilt

Possibly the Mite Society (Ladies' Aid), United Brethren Church

Center Point, Indiana

1900–1910

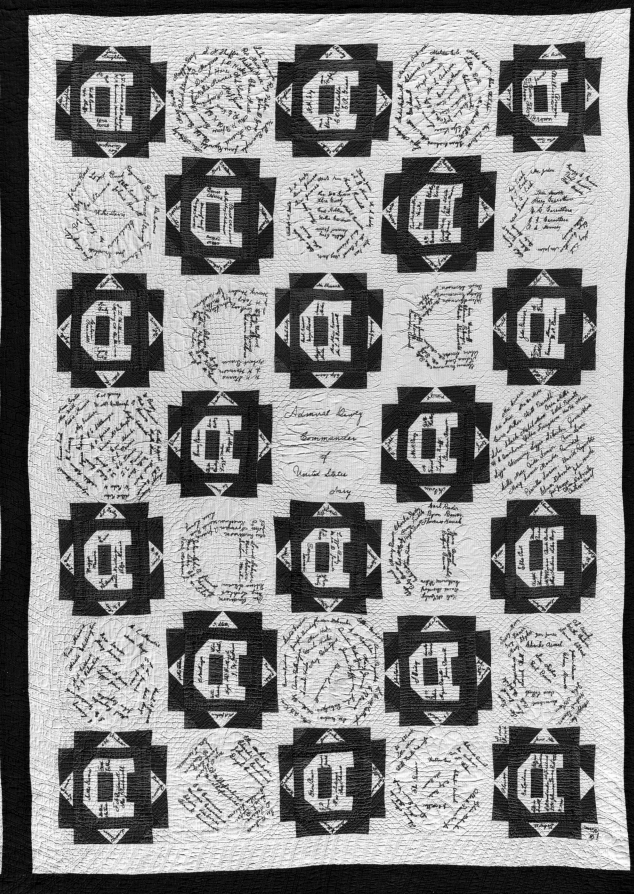

McKinley Community Church Signature Quilt

Ladies' Aid Society, McKinley Community Church

Warren, Ohio

Dated 1935

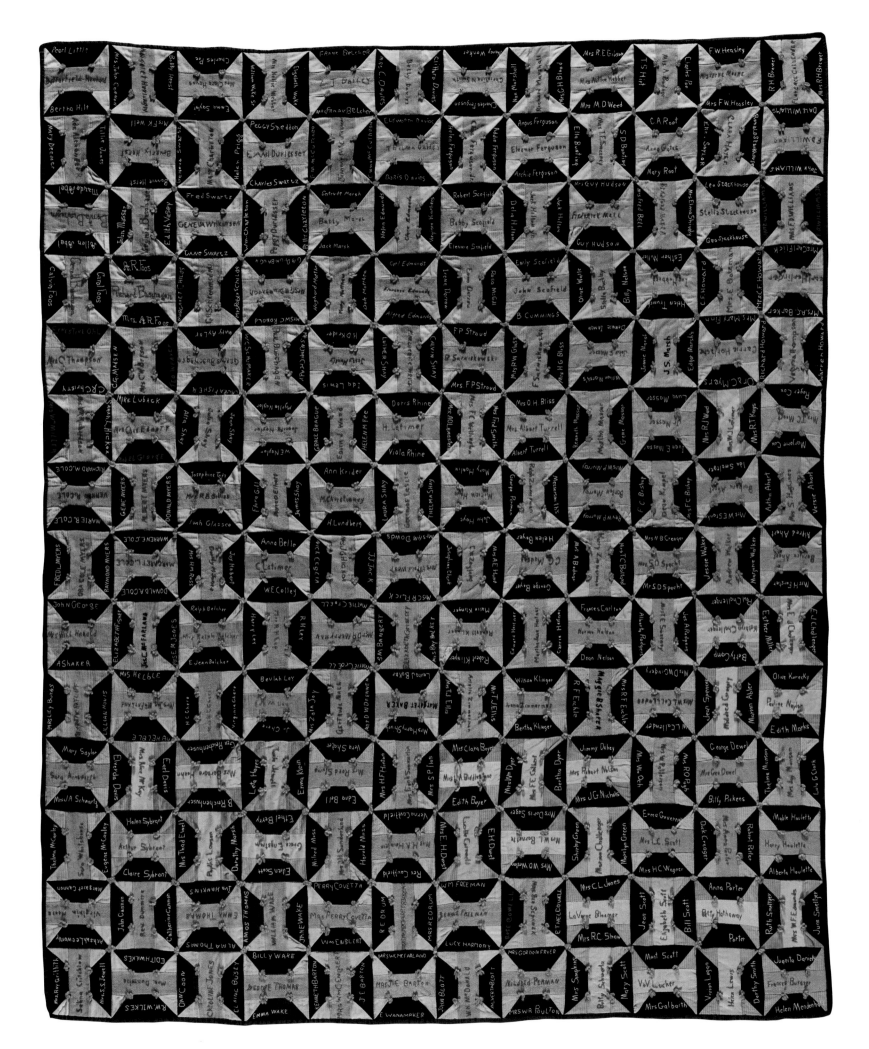

THE APPLIQUÉ QUILT

The rise in popularity in the 1840s of appliqué quilts has been traced to a number of factors, among them the fashion for album quilts (see previous chapter) and the widespread availability of relatively inexpensive cottons by the middle of the century. Signature album quilts of the early nineteenth century combined both conventional and cut-out chintz appliqué techniques. However, as the preference for block-style quilts over the center-medallion format increased, quiltmakers found that traditional chintz prints, which had a limited number of repeats that could be cut out, were less suited to individualized quilt blocks than the calicos and plain fabrics required for conventional appliqué.

Another important influence for the "new look" of appliqué quilts was the adoption of the quiltmaking tradition by Pennsylvania Germans. This conservative group of immigrants had long made their beds in the German style, sleeping under heavy home-woven ticks filled with straw and feathers. Beginning about 1830, however, they copied their English American neighbors and began making quilts that incorporated traditional German motifs,

including eight-lobed rosettes, three geometric flowers in a pot, hearts, birds, lilies, and tulips that are seen in many of the museum's floral appliqué quilts (pages 92–109), and this style came to dominate American appliqué quilts for the remainder of the century. Similarly, the red-and-green color scheme that is frequently found on floral appliqué bedcovers was a traditional color choice in many forms of Pennsylvania German folk art.

The museum's collection also contains a group of appliqué quilts that resemble the album quilts shown in the previous chapter but are believed to have been made by individual quiltmakers and do not belong to a tradition of group projects. As each block of these bedcovers is composed of a different pattern, they are often called "sampler appliqués" (pages 110–115). The *Bird of Paradise Quilt Top* (page 111), for example, named for the brightly plumed bird in the center, is arranged as a series of blocks containing floral and pictorial elements surrounded by a border. The figures on the quilt top were made using templates that were cut from newsprint and other papers dated from 1858 to 1863 and handed down with the bedcover (see page 110). Because this collection of template patterns includes the figure of a man who does not appear on the appropriate spot next to the figure of a woman on the quilt top, the bedcover may have been made in anticipation of a wedding that did not take place and for that reason was never quilted and completed.

Both the *Sarah Ann Garges Appliqué Bedcover* (page 117) and the *"Sacret Bibel" Quilt Top* (page 119) belong to long traditions of storytelling in fabric that are traceable to both Europe and Africa. According to family tradition, the Garges bedcover was made in celebration of the 1853 engagement of Sarah Ann Garges to Oliver Perry Shutt. It is decorated with scenes of traditional Pennsylvania Mennonite farm life arranged within and around a central diamond. Originally, there was a fourth figure of a man visible on this bedcover, but he was covered over with yellow fabric shaped to blend in with the rest of the motifs (see page 116). As the yellow fabric is the same as that used on the rest of the bedcover, the "cover-up" was probably done shortly after the quilt was completed. Why it was done, however, remains a mystery.

Information handed down with the *"Sacret Bibel" Quilt Top* stated that it, too, was made in Pennsylvania. The Susan Arrowood who signed this unusual bedcover is believed to have lived in West Chester, Pennsylvania, at the end of the nineteenth century. The scenes on the quilt top appear to have their origins in the Bible, although some may also represent activities at a church that was attended by the maker.

According to tradition, the final type of appliqué bedcover illustrated on these pages, the Hawaiian flag quilt (page 121), became popular in 1893, the year that Queen Liliuokalani was forced to abdicate her throne, which ultimately led to the annexation of the Hawaiian Islands to the United States. There is some evidence, however, that these flag quilts, known in Hawaiian as *Ku'u Hae Aloha* ("My Beloved Flag" or "Lost Beloved Flag"), were made as early as 1843, when the independent Kingdom of Hawaii was still considered a British protectorate. As seen in this example, Hawaiian quilts generally combine piecework with conventional appliqué techniques and intricate reverse appliqué.

Turkey Tracks Quilt

Artist unidentified

Possibly Ohio

1840–1850

"MTD" Quilt Top

Artist unidentified, appliquéd initials "MTD"

United States

Dated 1842

The Appliqué Quilt

Floral Crib Quilt

Artist unidentified

United States

1850–1880

Whig Rose Quilt

Abigail Hill (dates unknown)

Probably Indiana

Dated 1857–1858

Whig Rose Quilt with Swag and Tassel Border

Artist unidentified

United States

1850–1860

Whig Rose Quilt

Artist unidentified

Possibly Pennsylvania

1860–1880

Sunflowers Quilt

Artist unidentified

Possibly Pennsylvania

1860–1880

Sunflowers and Hearts Quilt

Artist unidentified

Possibly New England

1860–1880

Oak Leaves with Cherries Quilt

Artist unidentified

United States

1870–1880

The Appliqué Quilt

Centennial Quilt

Possibly Gertrude Knappenberger (dates unknown)

Possibly Emmaus, Pennsylvania

Dated 1876

Patterns for Bird of Paradise Quilt Top

Artist unidentified

Vicinity of Albany, New York

1858–1863

Bird of Paradise Quilt Top

Artist unidentified

Vicinity of Albany, New York

1858–1863

Union and Liberty Sampler Quilt

Artist unidentified

New York State

1860–1870

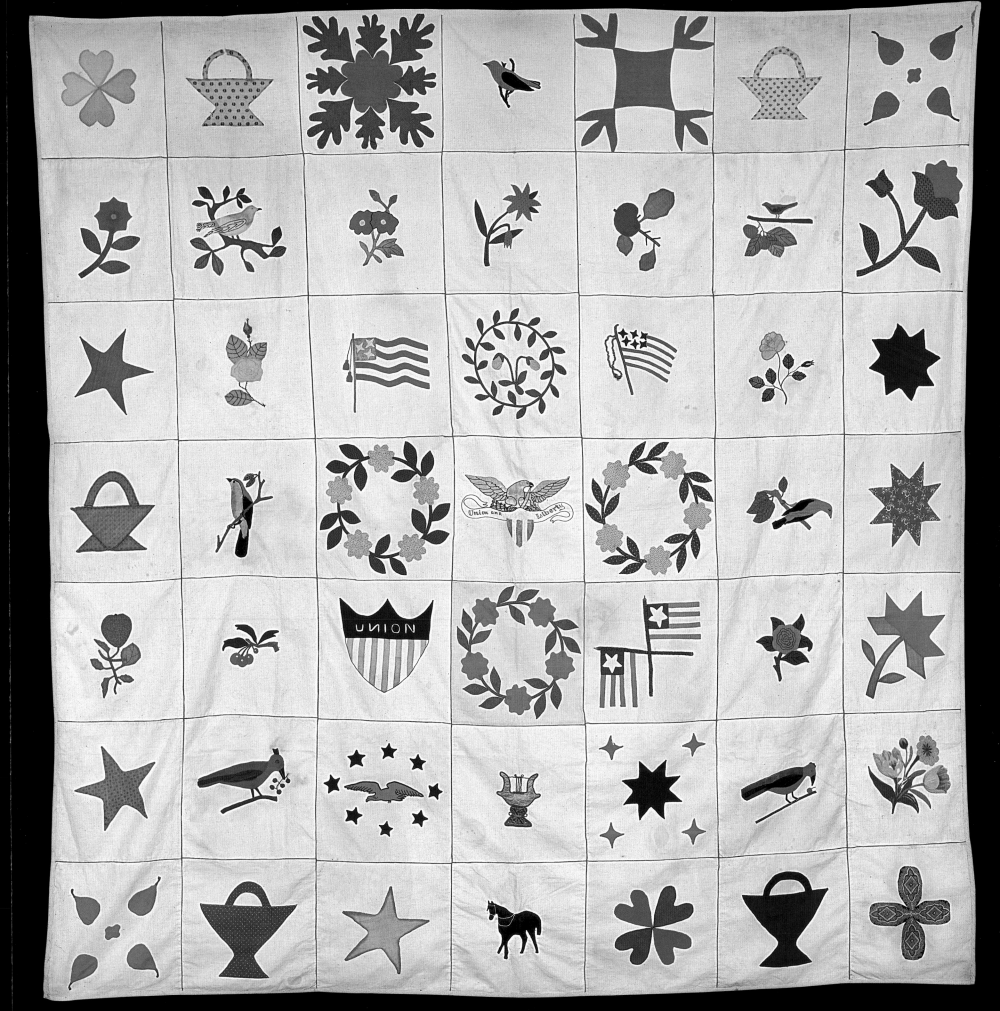

Cookie Cutter Quilt

Artist unidentified

Probably Pennsylvania

1875–1925

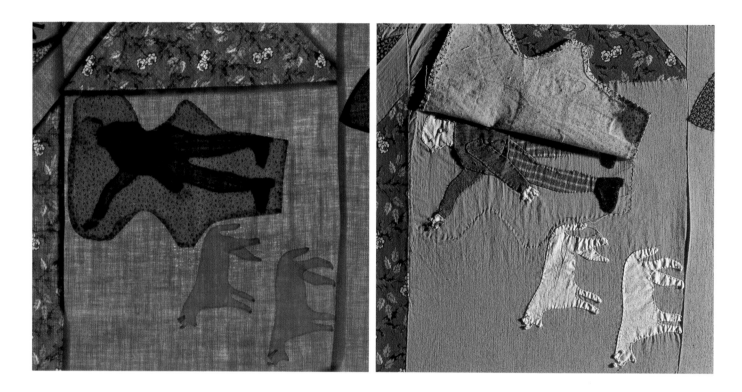

Details of Sarah Ann Garges Appliqué Bedcover

Male figure beneath cover-up (quilt back and quilt front,

appliqué uncovered)

Sarah Ann Garges Appliqué Bedcover

Sarah Ann Garges (c. 1834–c. 1887)

Doylestown, Pennsylvania

Dated 1853

Orange Peel Variation Quilt

Artist unidentified

Pennsylvania

1860–1880

Hawaiian Flag Quilt

Mother of Mina Ferguson (dates unknown)

Hawaii

1860–1870

THE PIECED QUILT

By the middle of the nineteenth century, quiltmaking in America was in full bloom. Particularly popular was the almost infinite variety of quilt patterns that could be devised based on geometric designs. Squares, rectangles, diamonds, triangles, and circles could be combined and recombined by quiltmakers in a multitude of traditional or original ways, and most were created using the technique of piecing, or "piecework." In this method of quiltmaking, designs are created out of fabrics that are seamed together side by side rather than layered on top of one another as they are in the various types of appliqué work.

Pieced-quilt designs range from basic arrangements of geometric pieces, such as in the *Four-Patch Quilt* (page 141) and the *Diamonds Quilt* (page 143), to intricate examples of a needleworker's skill. The maker of the *Charm Quilt* (page 144), for example, had to sew together hundreds of tiny squares of fabric—the goal was to create a quilt with no two matching pieces, a fad during the last quarter of the nineteenth century—to complete her bedcover. Doll quilts (page 147) were

often scaled-down versions of larger patterns and were frequently made by girls learning to sew.

Many star and "feathered" designs require a great deal of expertise to ensure that the pieces lay flat and do not pucker when sewn together. The *Pieties Quilt* (page 124), the *Feathered Touching Stars Quilt* (page 125), and the *"ECB" Feathered Stars Quilt* (page 127) have all been expertly pieced and enhanced with delicate quilting stitches, indicating that they may be representative of their makers' best work. The *Pieties Quilt*, however, is singular in its combination of pieced red and white fabric enhanced with biblical and secular homilies.

In general, piecing was favored for geometric patterns, although, as seen in the *Saddlebred Horse Quilt* (page 153), the technique could be adapted for pictorial designs as well. Patriotic themes, common in American quilts since the early years of the nation, were also popular in pieced quilts. Needleworkers have long expressed their national pride through specific motifs such as eagles, flags, and shields, as well as various combinations of the Stars and Stripes, and by incorporating printed commemorative fabrics into their bedcovers. Both the *Baby Crib Quilt* (page 148) and the *Flag Quilt* (page 149) were clearly inspired by the design of the American flag. The *Baby Crib Quilt* is an adaptation of an illustration that was published in *Peterson's Magazine* in June 1861 under the caption "A Patriotic Quilt." The thirty-four stars in its center represent the states of the Union, both North and South, at the time and probably imply that the maker held Union sentiments.

The *Abraham Lincoln Flag Quilt* (page 150) and the *Grover Cleveland Quilt* (page 152) commemorate past presidents of the United States. Cleveland's portrait in the center of the *Grover Cleveland Quilt*, which was pieced in a light-and-dark pattern resembling the Barn Raising set of some Log Cabin quilts (see next chapter), was probably taken from a flag banner used in Cleveland's 1884 presidential campaign or from a red pocket handkerchief or bandanna that was one of the symbols of his 1888 reelection campaign. The portrait of Lincoln, however, was embroidered in the center of the other bedcover, whose design was inspired by the American flag.

Little acts of kindness
Little words of love

Make our earthly eden
like our Heaven above

Is our
Home a
Heaven

Heaven
is our
Home

Be still Peace

Kind
words
Never
Die

Forgive
as you
hope to be
forgiven

Earth has
no sorrow
Heaven
cannot
heal

Be still
and know
that I am
God

No cross
No crown

Thy will
be done

Oh sacred
Patience
with my
soul abide

There is a
magic in
kindness
that springs
from above

Maria
Cadman
Hubbard
aged 79

If you can
not be a
Golden pipp
in don't turn
crab apple

With us

Love one
another

1848

Feathered Touching Stars Quilt

Artist unidentified

Ohio

Dated 1846

Pieties Quilt

Maria Cadman Hubbard (possibly 1769–?)

Probably Austerlitz, New York

Dated 1848

Star of Bethlehem with Star Border Quilt

Artist unidentified

United States

1840–1860

"ECB" Feathered Stars Quilt

Artist unidentified, pieced initials "ECB"

Possibly New York State

1850–1860

The Pieced Quilt

Baskets Quilt

Artist unidentified

United States

1840–1860

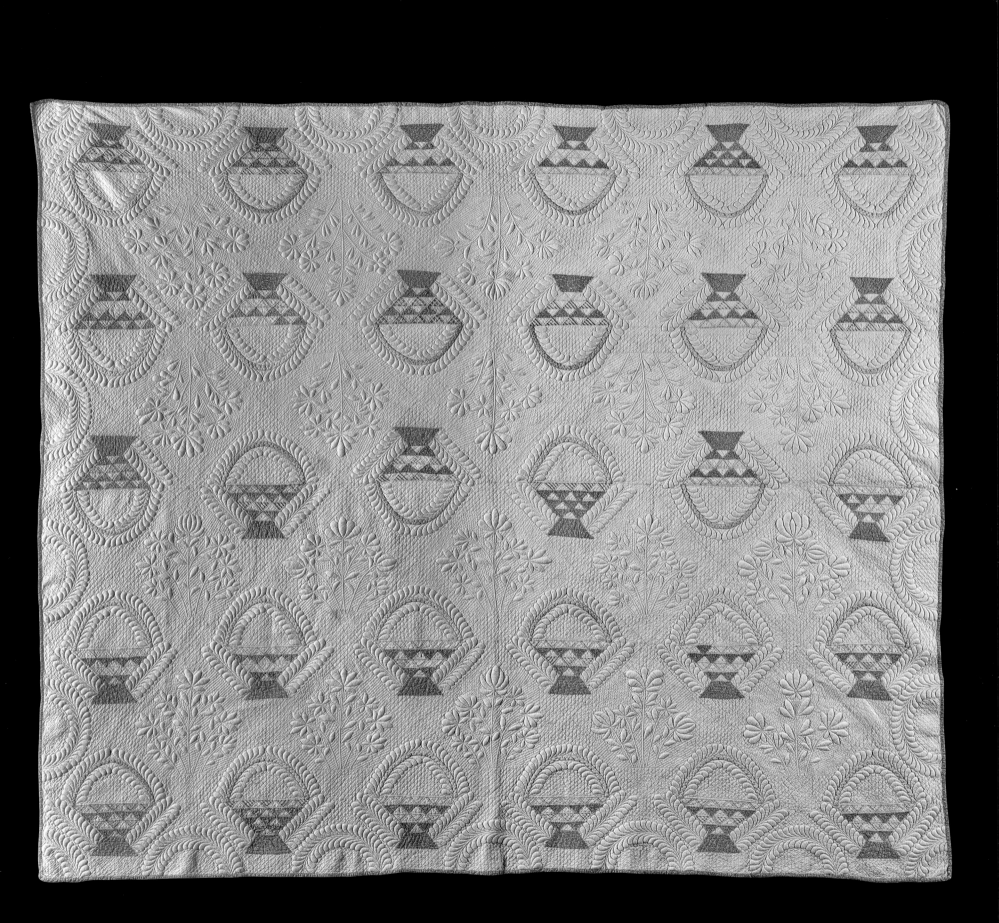

Pieced Block-Work Quilt with Printed Border

Artist unidentified

Pennsylvania

1840–1860

Pennsylvania Hex Quilt

Artist unidentified

United States

1860–1900

Stars Quilt

Unidentified member of the Hemiup Family

Geneva, New York

1860–1900

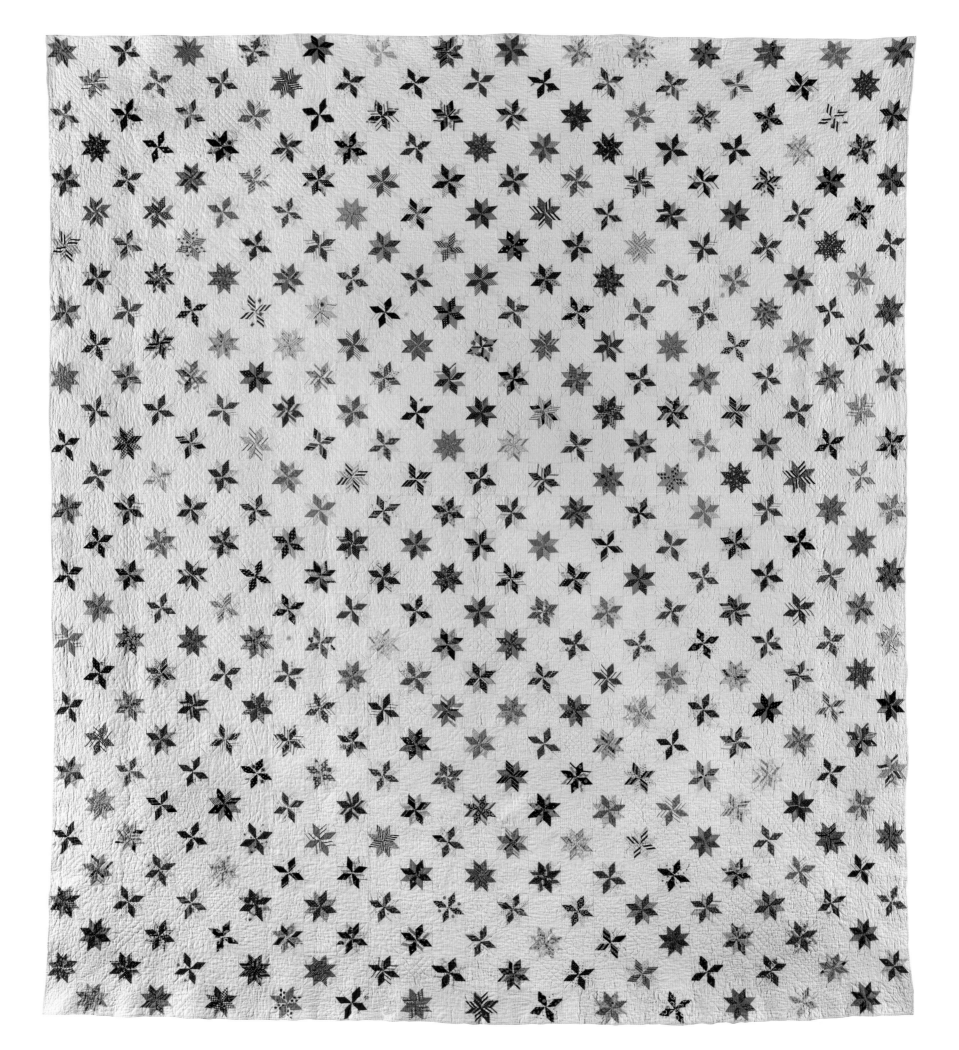

Slashed Star Quilt

Sara Maartz (dates unknown)

Lancaster, Pennsylvania

Dated 1872

Indian Pine Quilt

Artist unidentified, embroidered initials "BB"

Maine

1880–1890

Triangles and Flying Geese Quilt

Artist unidentified

United States

1875–1900

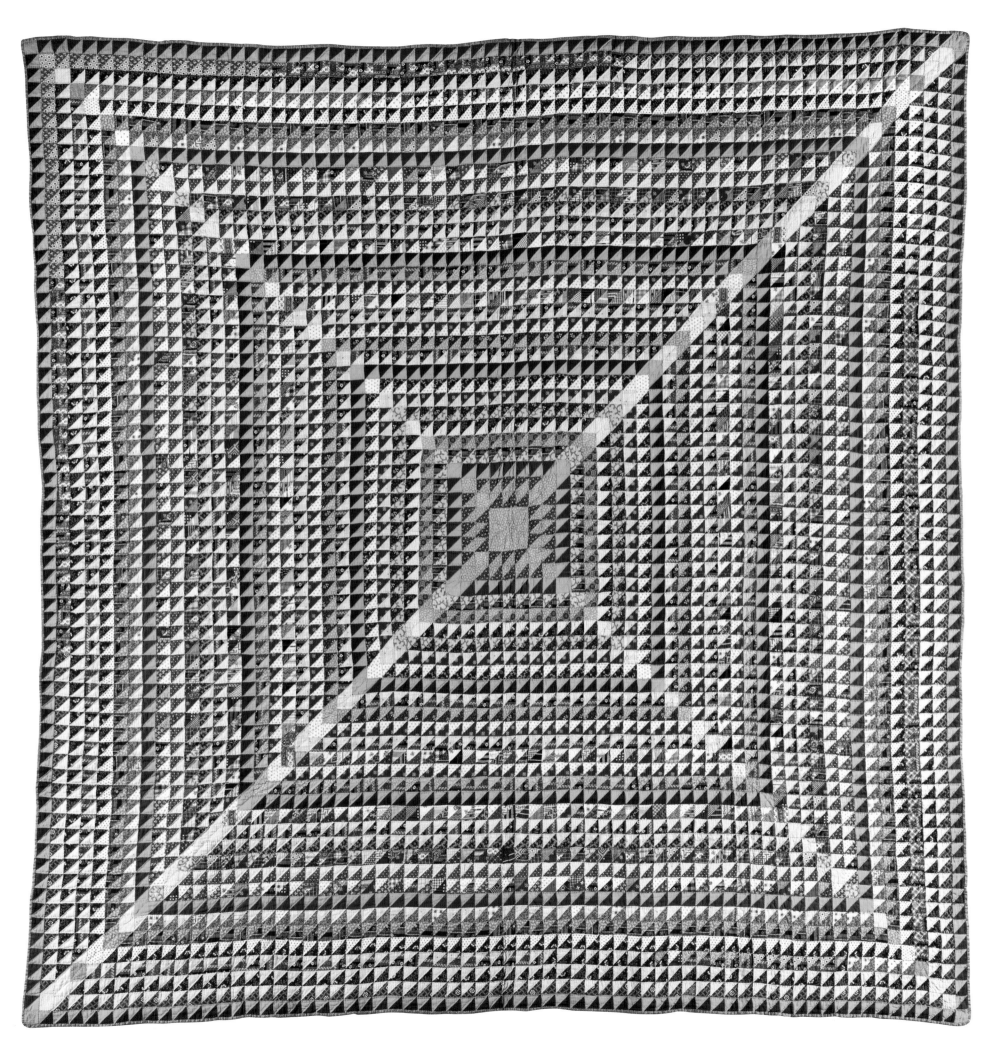

Cross and Block Quilt

Artist unidentified

Possibly New York State, Pennsylvania, or Ontario

1880–1900

Double T Quilt

Artist unidentified

Possibly New York State, Pennsylvania, or Ontario

1880–1900

Four-Patch Quilt

Artist unidentified

United States

1880–1900

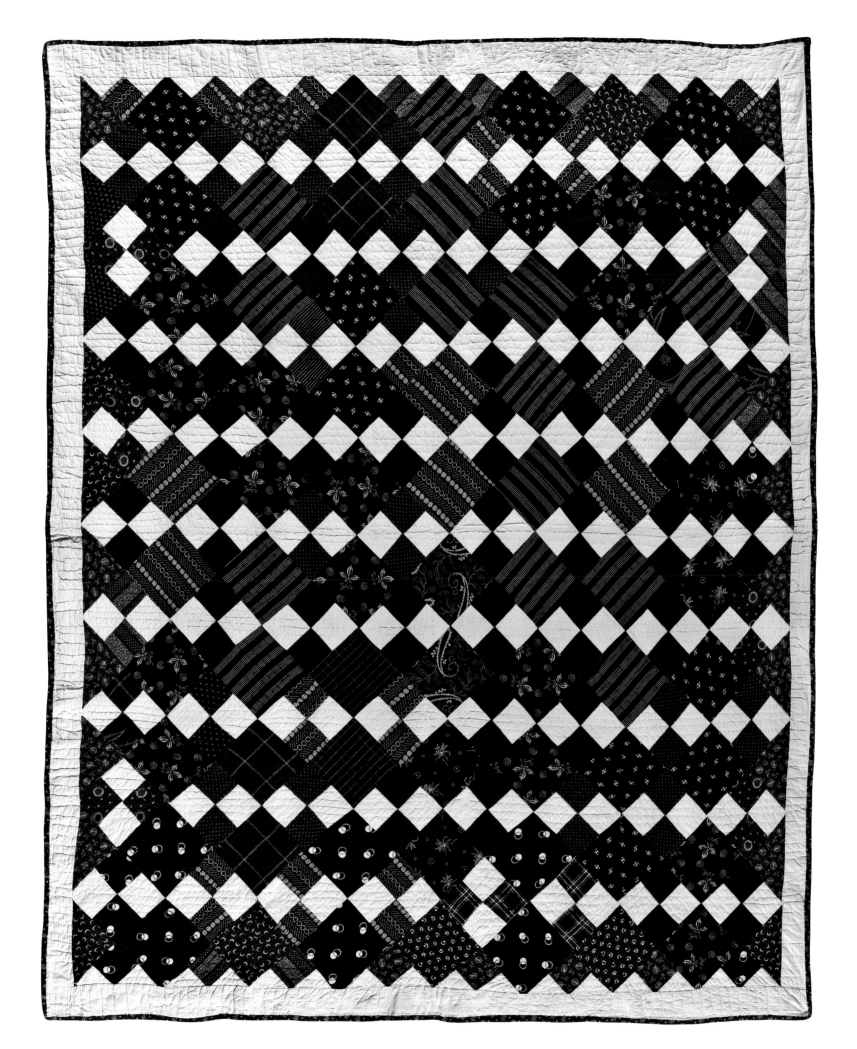

Diamonds Quilt

Artist unidentified

Possibly New York State, Pennsylvania, or Ontario

1880–1910

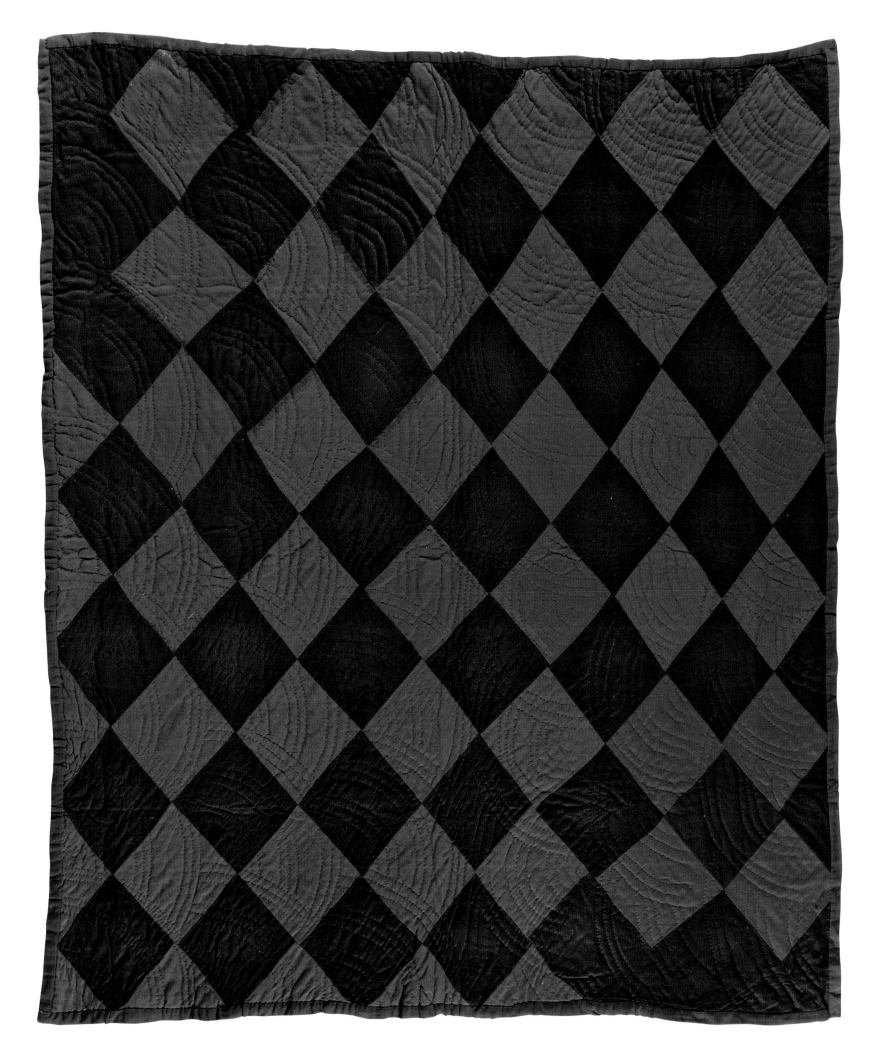

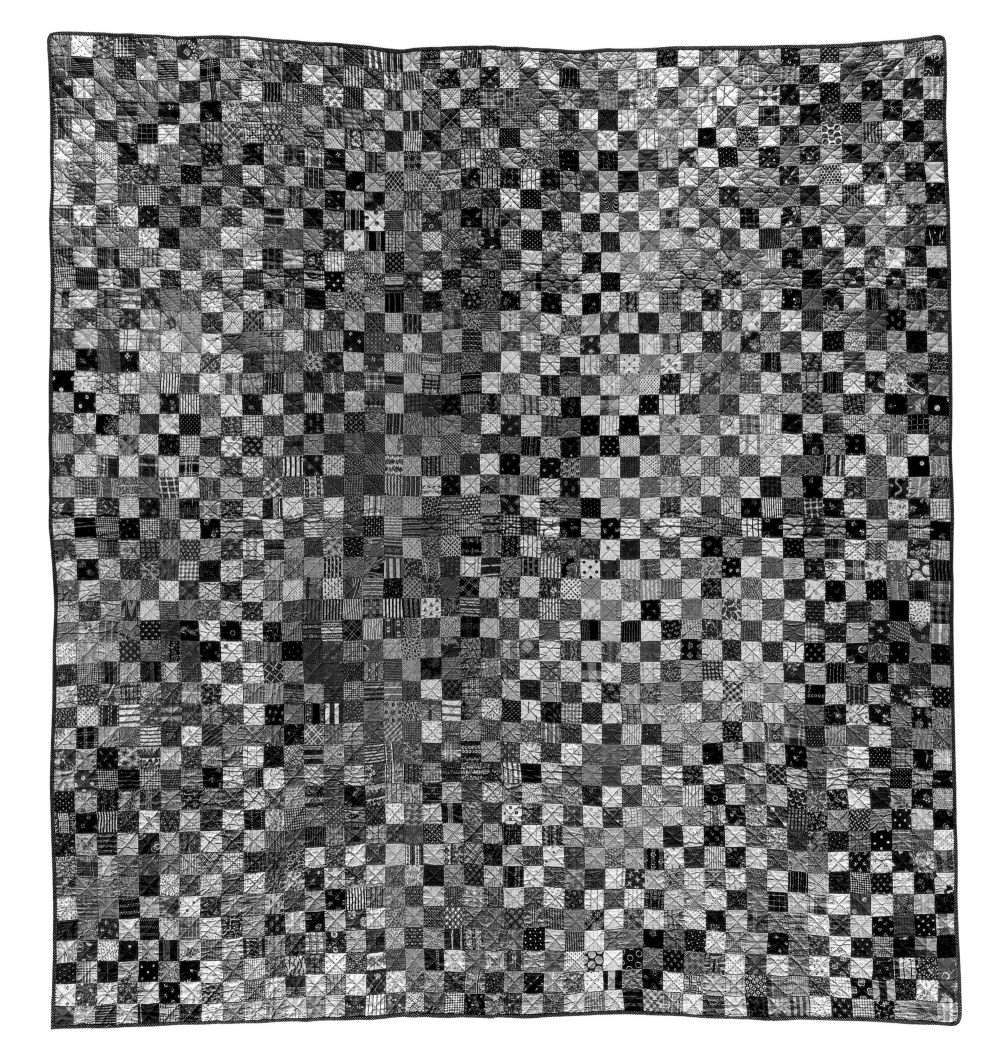

Charm Quilt

Artist unidentified

United States

1880–1920

Roman Cross Quilt

Artist unidentified

United States

1900–1920

Ohio Star Crib Quilt

Artist unidentified

United States

1920–1940

Collection of Doll Quilts

Artists unidentified

United States

1880–1960

Baby Crib Quilt

Artist unidentified

Possibly Kansas

1861–1875

Flag Quilt

Mary C. Baxter (dates unknown)

Kearny, New Jersey

1898–1910

Abraham Lincoln Flag Quilt

Lucy Frost (dates unknown)

Iowa

1866

Grover Cleveland Quilt

Artist unidentified

New York State

1884–1890

Saddlebred Horse Quilt

Artist unidentified

Possibly Kentucky

1910–1930

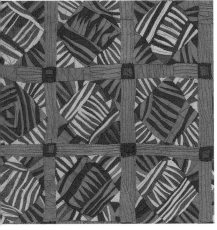

THE LOG CABIN QUILT

The Log Cabin quilt has often been described as the archetypal American bedcover. There is even some evidence to support a North American origin for the design: in England, where the American quiltmaking tradition originated, this type of piecing is generally known as "American patchwork." The Log Cabin tradition is also important in American textile history because it introduced a new method of construction that was different from both the American (running-stitch) and English (paper-template) piecing techniques that were popular previously. Known as "foundation patchwork" or "foundation piecing," or sometimes "pressed piecing," the method calls for the individual pieces of fabric, in this case the logs of the cabin, to be sewn to an underlying piece of fabric, or foundation, as well as to one another. The resulting bedcovers are usually so heavy that a separate filling or batting is not needed, and they are usually not quilted, though some may be tied with knotted thread to ensure all the layers hold together. This foundation method of piecing is also used for the Crazy quilts and Fan and String quilts,

which became popular after the Log Cabin quilts had been developed.

The great enthusiasm for the pattern, dating from its origins in the 1860s, is probably attributable to its immense versatility: many varieties of Log Cabin quilts have been created, almost all of which are based on the principle of individual blocks composed of half light strips and half dark strips of fabric. The Barn Raising variation (pages 156–161), for example, features blocks that are divided by color diagonally, while the Courthouse Steps pattern (pages 162–167) is composed of blocks that have colors arranged horizontally and vertically. Thus, the overall pattern of the quilt is determined by the way in which the separate blocks are sewn together.

At some point in the mid- to late 1870s, a variation of the basic Log Cabin design known as the Windmill Blades, or Pineapple, pattern (pages 169–173) became popular among American quiltmakers. In this variation of the Log Cabin design, the darker fabrics are usually arranged to form "blades," or "pineapples," that radiate from the center squares. The ends of all the strips are clipped at an angle to create the illusion of motion, or to suggest the spiky leaves of a pineapple. Assembling this pattern is often more complex than for the other Log Cabin designs and requires great precision in the piecing.

Most of the Log Cabin quilts in the museum's collection were not made as functional bedcovers and therefore fall into the "show quilt" tradition of the late nineteenth century (see next chapter). These quilts were made of luxurious fabrics, primarily silks, including velvet and satin, and were intended as parlor throws or spreads or for other decorative uses. A typical example is the *Log Cabin Throw, Light-and-Dark Variation* (page 175),

a relatively small textile made of strips of silk ties and velvet.

The final quilt highlighted in this chapter, the *String Quilt* (page 176), is included here because, in terms of both design and construction, string quilts generally resemble Log Cabins more than any other type of quilt. String quilts, made of many pieces of narrow fabric sewn together, became popular in the last quarter of the nineteenth century and continued to be made well into the twentieth century. Like Log Cabin quilts, they were usually foundation pieced. Log Cabins made after 1920, however, generally were constructed using the traditional American running-stitch piecing method.

Log Cabin Quilt, Barn Raising Variation

Mary Jane Smith (1833–1869) and

Mary Morrell Smith (1798–1869)

Whitestone, New York

1861–1865

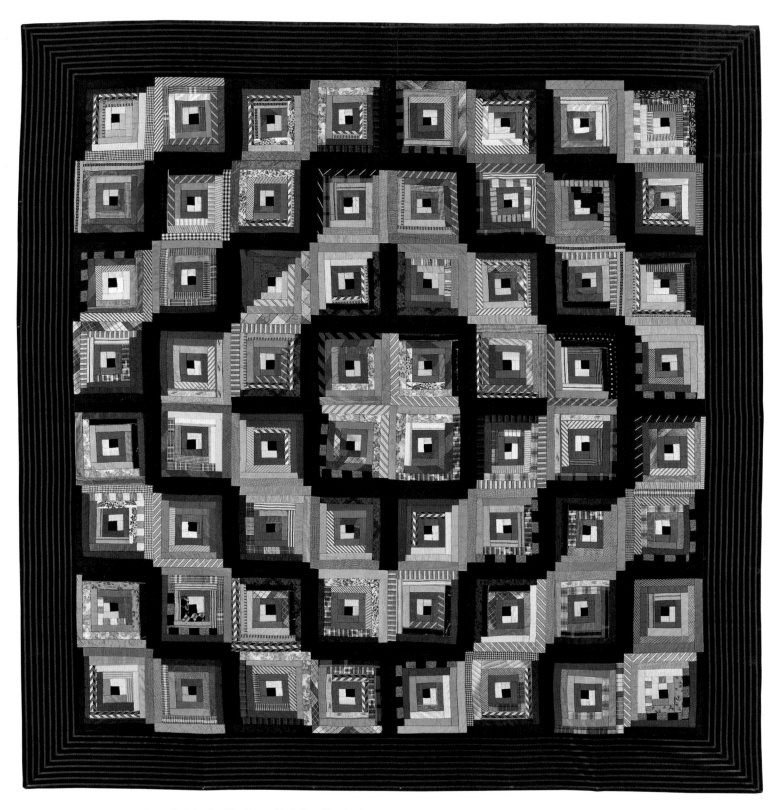

Log Cabin Quilt, Barn Raising Variation

Sarah Olmstead King (dates unknown)

Connecticut

1875–1885

Log Cabin Quilt, Barn Raising Variation

Artist unidentified

United States

Dated 1887

Log Cabin Quilt, Barn Raising Variation

Unidentified Mennonite artist

Ohio

1950–1960

Log Cabin Quilt, Courthouse Steps Variation

Artist unidentified

United States

1870–1890

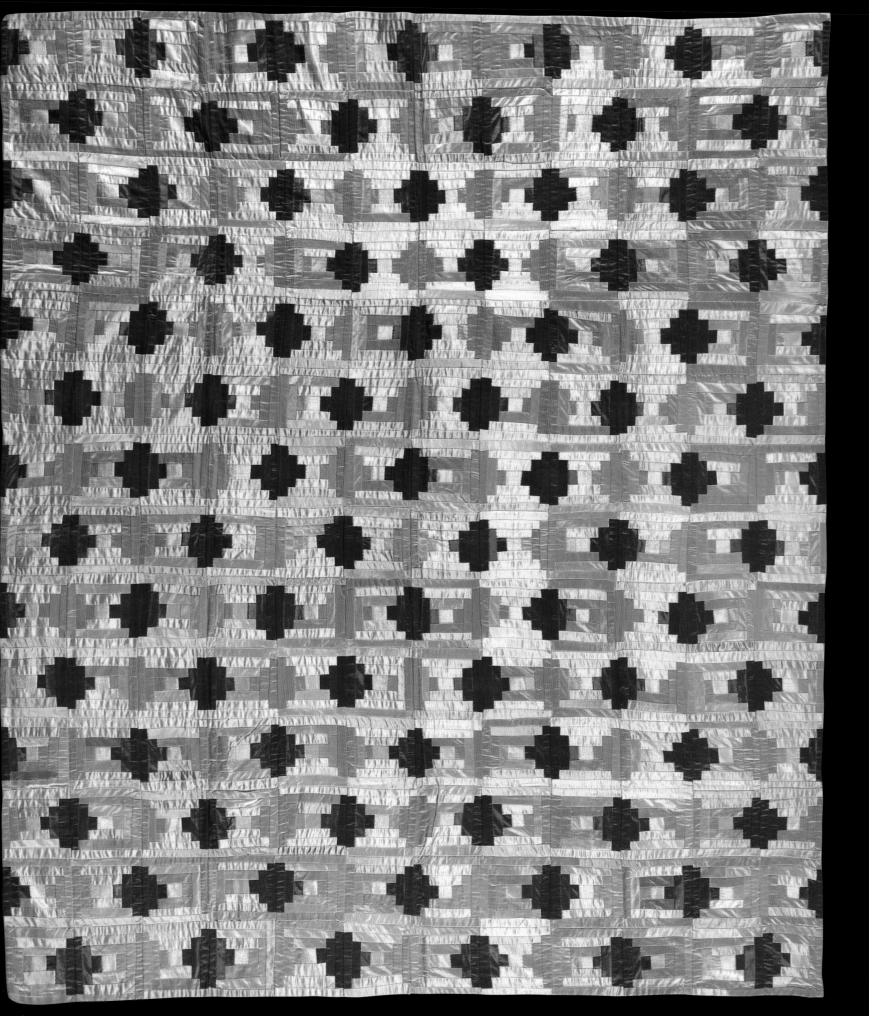

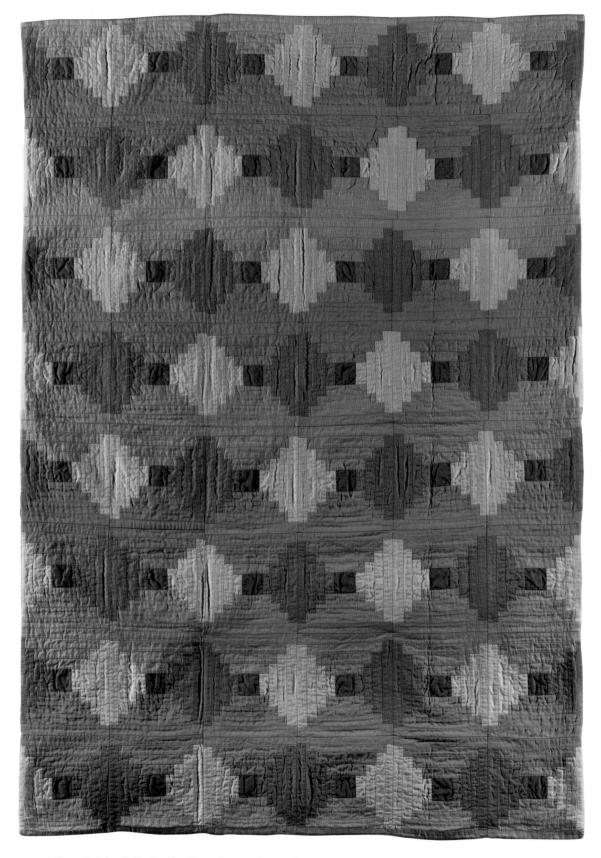

Log Cabin Crib Quilt, Courthouse Steps Variation

Artist unidentified

United States

1920–1950

Log Cabin Quilt, Courthouse Steps Variation

Samuel Steinberger (1865–c. 1934)

New York City

1890–1910

Log Cabin Quilt, Windmill Blades Variation

Artist unidentified

United States

1885–1920

Log Cabin Throw, Light-and-Dark Variation

Harriet Rutter Eagleson (1855–c. 1925)

New York City

1874–1880

String Quilt

Artist unidentified

Possibly Kentucky

1920–1940

THE SHOW QUILT

Although they are called quilts, the textiles in this chapter were not meant to be used as functional bedcovers and generally were neither composed of a traditional quilt's three layers (top, filling, backing) nor quilted. One might be placed on a bed for decorative effect or draped over the back of a sofa, but never was it slept under, laundered, or treated like its utilitarian cotton cousin. Rather, a show quilt, usually made of delicate silk or fine wool, was intended to demonstrate its maker's good taste and her knowledge of popular decorative trends.

By the middle of the nineteenth century, silk—once too rare and expensive for the average quiltmaker—had become both attainable and affordable due to the expansion of the China trade and began to replace cotton for dresses and quilts among the most stylish. At this time, a silk show quilt style developed parallel to the calico quilt tradition. The *Star of Bethlehem Quilt* (page 181) and the *Variable Stars Quilt* (page 184) are examples of show quilts made entirely of silk but in patterns that could—and probably thirty years earlier would—have been made of cotton.

Crazy quilts were not only the most popular form of show quilts but possibly the most popular of all American quilts. The Crazy quilt era is generally dated from 1876, the year of the Philadelphia Centennial Exposition, to the beginning of the twentieth century; 1884 was the peak year for Crazies in contemporary periodicals. The Exposition introduced Americans to the principles of the Aesthetic movement, art needlework, and Japanese design, all elements that contributed to the distinctive look of Crazy quilts.

Many show quilts have erroneously been cataloged as Crazy quilts in the past, and although they often share some of the same characteristics as Crazies, such as foundation piecing, luxurious fabrics, and embroidery embellishments, they were not randomly patched and should not be categorized with the true Crazies. The *Stars and Pentagons Quilt* (page 186), for example, has a number of asymmetrical features and an appearance of irregularity but is actually composed of a regular pattern of pieced pentagons and five-pointed stars. Similarly, the *Map Quilt* (page 189), while at first glance seemingly displaying the irregular patchwork typical of Crazies, in fact features the outlines of the forty-eight contiguous states, some decorated with embroidery flourishes, set against a regular background known as "right-angle piecing."

True Crazy quilts vary from unusual examples such as the *Equestrian Crazy Quilt* (page 192), which combines Crazy piecing with appliquéd and embroidered figures on horseback, to the more commonplace. Even the most typical textiles in the category, however, usually include decorative details—embroidered, painted, or printed designs such as flowers, animals, or figures from popular literature—that distinguish one from another and individualize each maker's work. Examples illustrated here display motifs ranging from common Japanese-inspired designs, such as fans, butterflies, and owls, and depictions of children copied from the illustrated stories of Kate Greenaway (pages 194–197) to elaborately embroidered designs that show off the maker's needlework skills.

By the end of the nineteenth century, show quilts began to wane in popularity and be replaced by the cotton quilts of the Revival period (see next chapter). One type of bedcover that bridged the two styles was the outline embroidered quilt, represented here by the *In Honor Shall Wave Spread* (page 200). Outline embroidery was already in use on the elaborate Crazies and other show quilts of the 1880s and 1890s, and many of the designs could be found in books and magazines. The maker of this textile, however, expanded her repertoire by drawing from sources as diverse as Currier & Ives prints and Kate Greenaway drawings.

**Appliquéd and Embroidered
Pictorial Bedcover**

Artist unidentified

Possibly New York State

1825–1845

Star of Bethlehem Quilt

Artist unidentified

Possibly Sullivan County, New York

1880–1900

Soldier's Quilt

Artist unidentified

Probably United States, Canada, or Great Britain

1854–1890

Variable Stars Quilt

Artist unidentified

United States

1880–1900

**Oregon Pioneer Organization
Quilt for Euda Aletha Kelly**

Eudoxia Aurora Kelly Niblin (1865–1945)

Oregon

Dated 1923

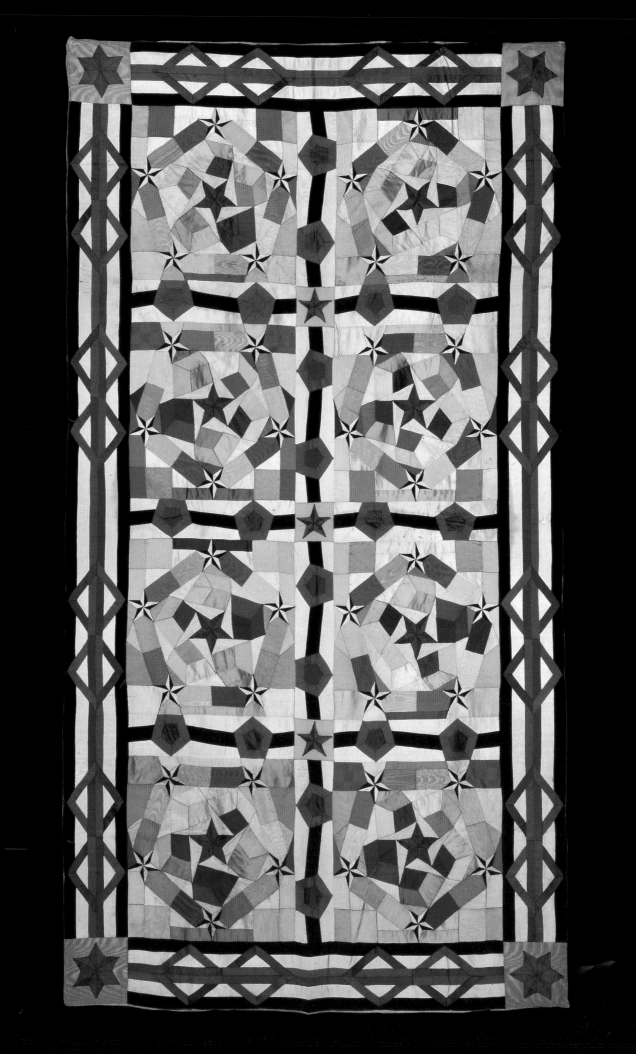

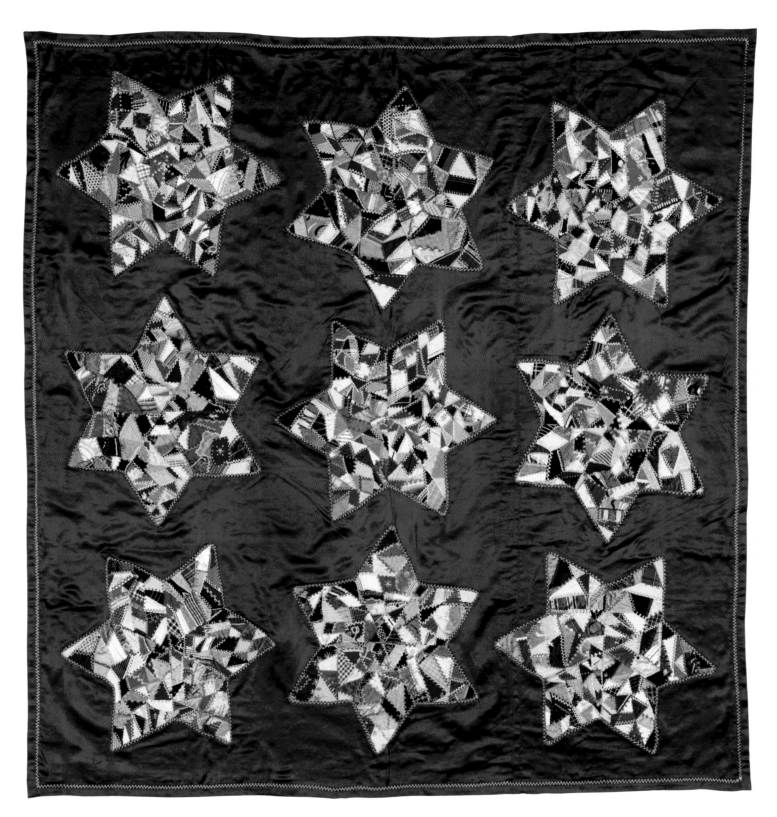

Stars and Pentagons Quilt

Artist unidentified

United States

1880–1900

Show Quilt with Contained Crazy Stars

Unidentified member of the McAllister Family

Barnstead, New Hampshire

1885–1920

Map Quilt

Artist unidentified

Possibly Virginia

1886

Crazy Quilt Top

Angelina Grattan (dates unknown)

United States

1880–1890

Center Star Crazy Throw

Mary Ann Crocker Hinman (1817–1893)

New York State

1880–1890

Cleveland-Hendricks Crazy Quilt

Artist unidentified, initialed "J.F.R."

United States

1885–1890

Equestrian Crazy Quilt

Artist unidentified

Possibly New York State

1880–1900

Crazy Quilt

Rachel Blair Greene (1846–1909)

Belvedere, New Jersey

1885–1895

"S.H." Crazy Quilt

Artist unidentified, initialed "S.H."

United States

1885–1895

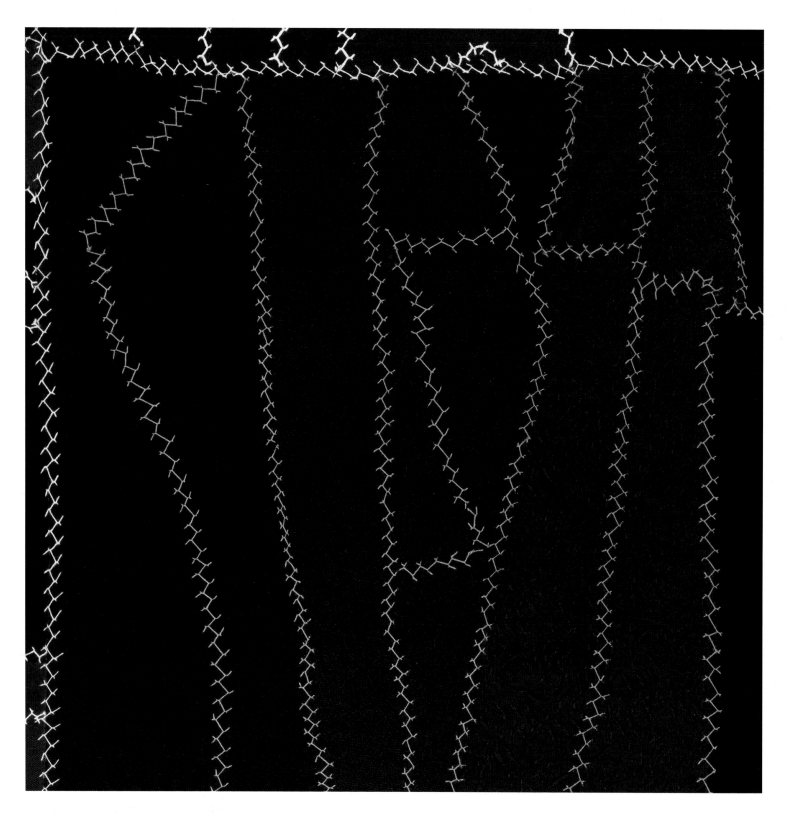

"Ella" Crazy Quilt

Artist unidentified, embroidered "Ella"

United States

Dated 1922

In Honor Shall Wave Spread

Artist unidentified

THE REVIVAL QUILT

Popular interest in the American past was sparked by the Philadelphia Centennial Exposition of 1876 and encouraged by the spread of the Arts and Crafts movement in the late nineteenth century. Proponents of Arts and Crafts urged housewives to throw away their clutter and heavy drapes and to have nothing in their home that they did not know to be useful or believe to be beautiful. They promoted natural, unadorned materials, good workmanship, and simple designs. Advocates of this new, "cleaner" decorating style championed cotton quilts, which had been made before silk show quilts became fashionable, and by the 1880s, some publications were already forecasting the end of the silk show quilt fad.

While an interest in old quilts was ignited by the Arts and Crafts movement, it was the Colonial Revival of the early twentieth century that truly inspired women to search their attics and basements for antique quilts and, failing that, to sew their own interpretations of the old-time bedcovers. Museum exhibitions, magazine articles, and even advertisements for household products encouraged Americans to decorate in what

was becoming the unofficial national style, and cotton patchwork quilts were viewed as the appropriate accessories for the new decorating mode that drew its inspiration from a romanticized American past. The *Tree of Life Cut-out Chintz Quilt* (page 207) was obviously inspired by textiles that had been popular in the late eighteenth and early nineteenth centuries (see pages 50–51) and even used antique fabrics for some of the motifs in its center.

The great enthusiasm between 1910 and 1950 for making quilts of colorful cotton fabrics owes much of its impetus to a talented group of women who provided original designs to a public that was fascinated with the handiwork of the American past yet eager to have their homes appear light, bright, and "modern." Some of these women were professional designers, others were talented amateurs who began designing their own quilts because of their dissatisfaction with the patterns of the past, and some toiled anonymously for the myriad pattern companies that catered to the enormous demand for new designs. Many of the textiles shown on the following pages were sewn using commercial patterns or kits that provided everything needed to complete a quilt, including the fabric; among them are the *Holly Hocks Quilt* (page 219), based on a Mountain Mist pattern from the 1930s, the *Kitten Appliqué Quilt* (page 227), a design published in newspapers under both the Alice Brooks and Laura Wheeler pseudonyms used by Needlecraft Service of New York, and the *Star of France Quilt* (page 229), an art deco design from Hubert Ver Mehren's Home Art Studios of Des Moines. A few patterns, such as Double Wedding Ring (pages 232–234) and Dresden Plate (page 238), became especially popular during this period and have come to epitomize the bright, cheery look that is today often associated with the term *quilt revival*.

Bull's Eye Quilt

Member of the family of Alverda H. (Hoffman) Herb

Berks County, Pennsylvania

1900–1920

Tree of Life Cut-out Chintz Quilt

Artist unidentified, initialed "GMR"

Probably Wiscasset, Maine

1925–1935

Trailing Ivy Quilt

Artist unidentified

United States

1930–1940

Apple Blossom Quilt

Ladies' Aid Society of the Methodist Church

Hoag's Corner, New York

1939–1945

Tulip and Rose Bouquet Quilt

Elizabeth Schumacher Leece (1867–1956)

Kansas City, Missouri

1930–1945

Basket of Flowers Quilt

Elizabeth Schumacher Leece (1867–1956)

Kansas City, Missouri

1930–1940

Daisy Rings Quilt

Elizabeth Schumacher Leece (1867–1956)

Kansas City, Missouri

1930–1945

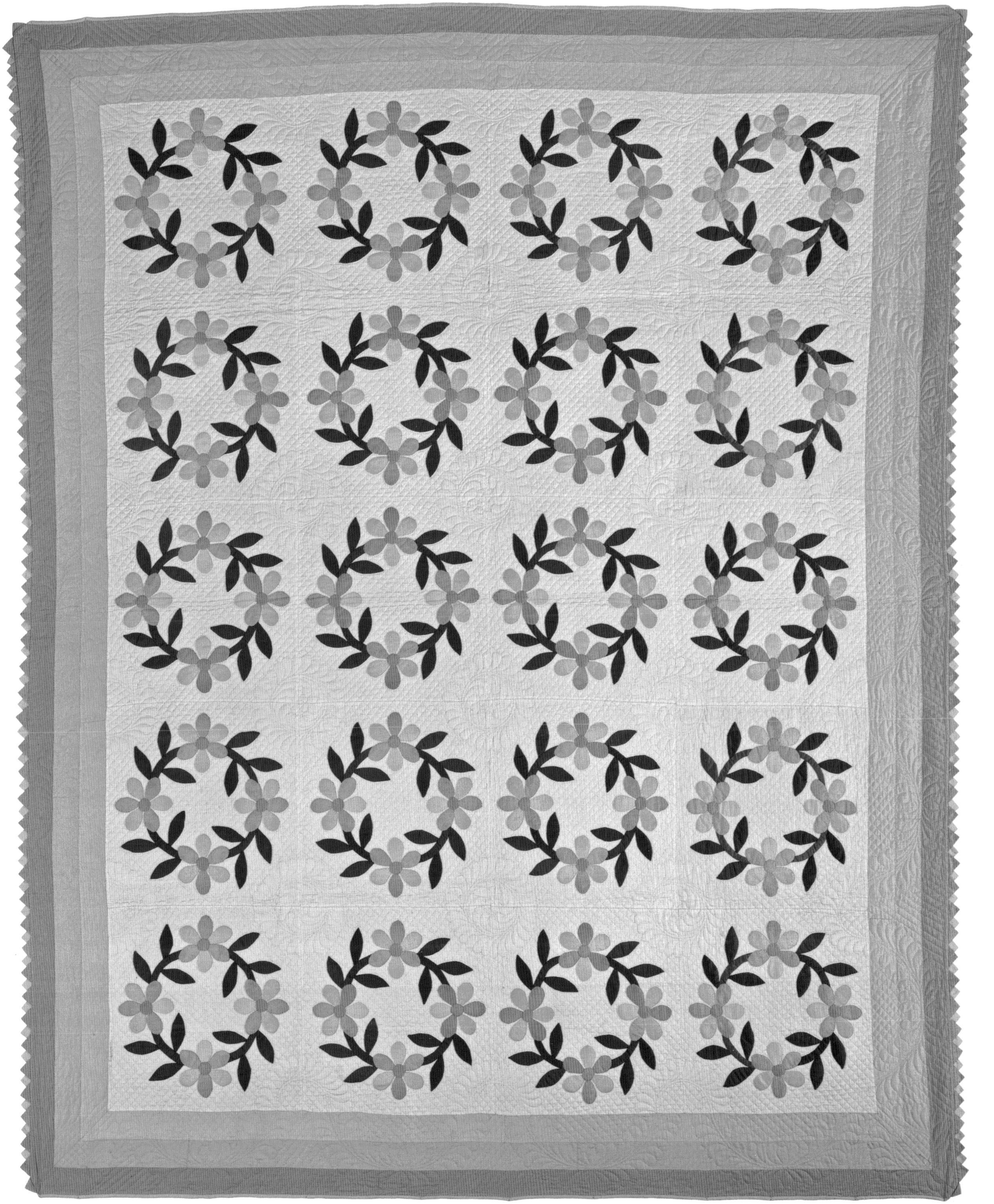

Pinwheel Sunflower Quilt

Mary Etta (Mrs. Edward Emmet) Bach (1872–1974)

Philadelphia

1930–1950

Ladies' Dream Quilt

Mary Etta (Mrs. Edward Emmet) Bach (1872–1974)

Philadelphia

1930–1940

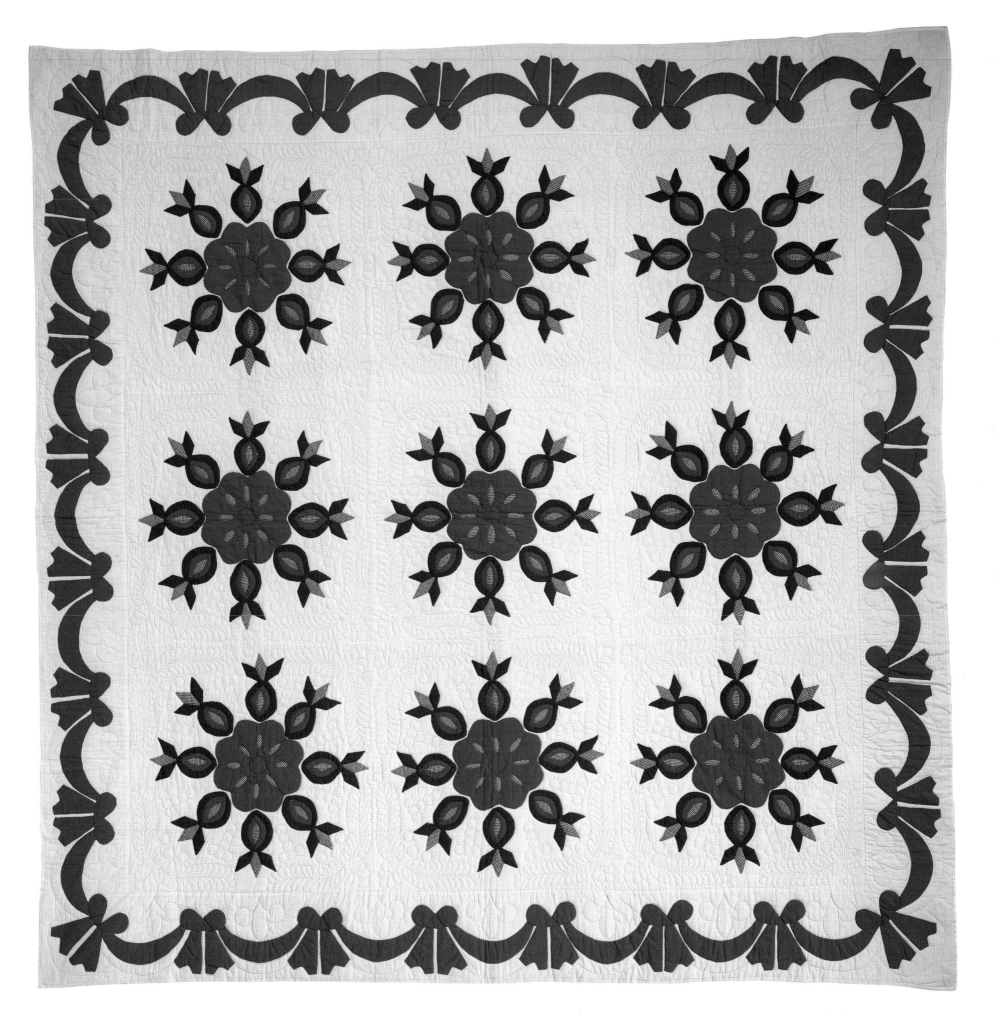

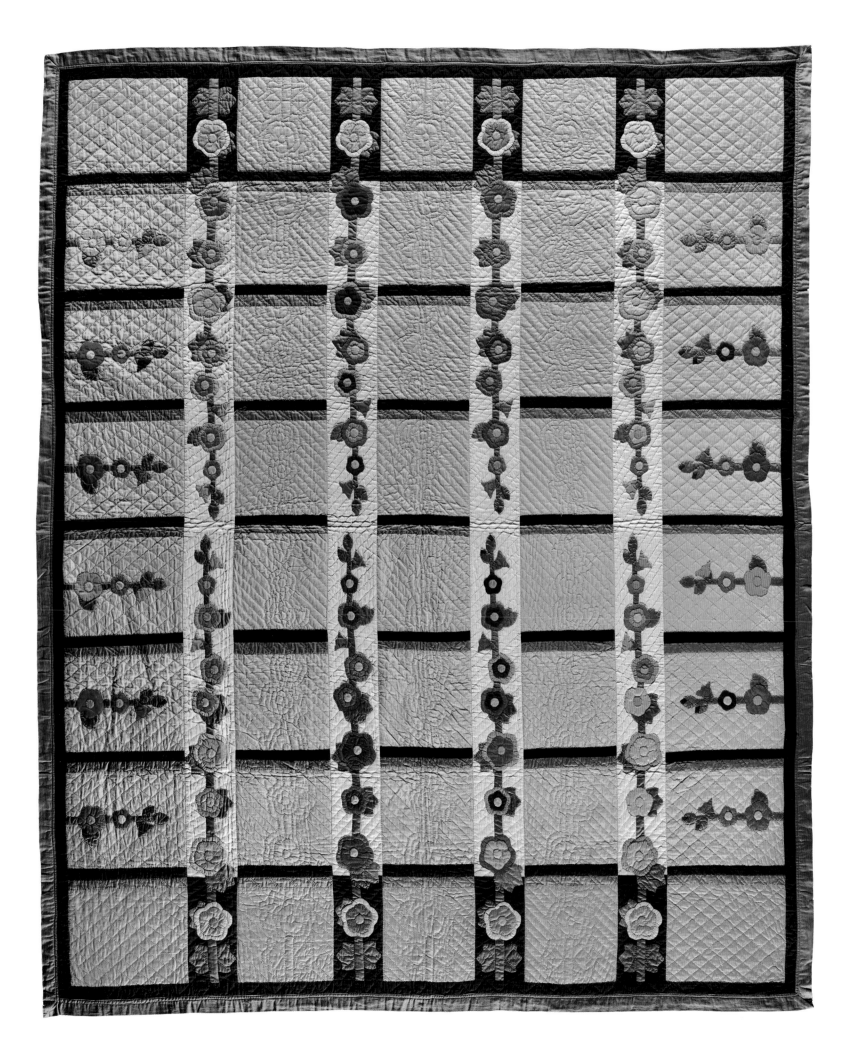

Roses and Ribbons Quilt

Artist unidentified

United States

1930–1940

English Flower Garden Quilt

Jennie Pingrey (Mrs. Charles O.) Stotts (c. 1861–?)

Yates Center, Kansas

1930–1935

Embroidered Floral Appliqué Quilt

Artist unidentified

United States

1930–1940

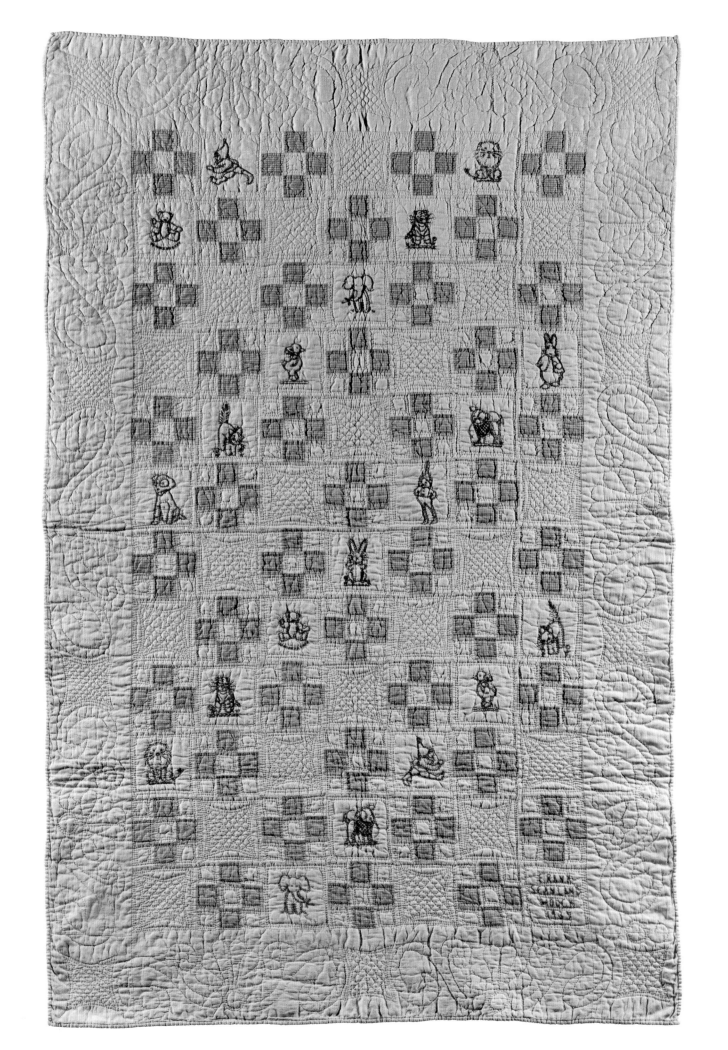

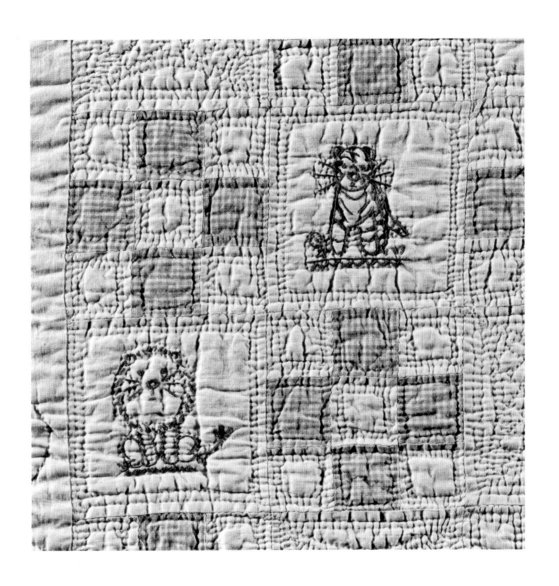

Outline Embroidered Child's Quilt

Artist unidentified

United States

Dated 1933

Gingham Dog and Calico Cat Crib Quilt

Artist unidentified

Probably Pennsylvania

1920–1930

Kitten Appliqué Quilt

Artist unidentified

Possibly Kentucky

1941–1950

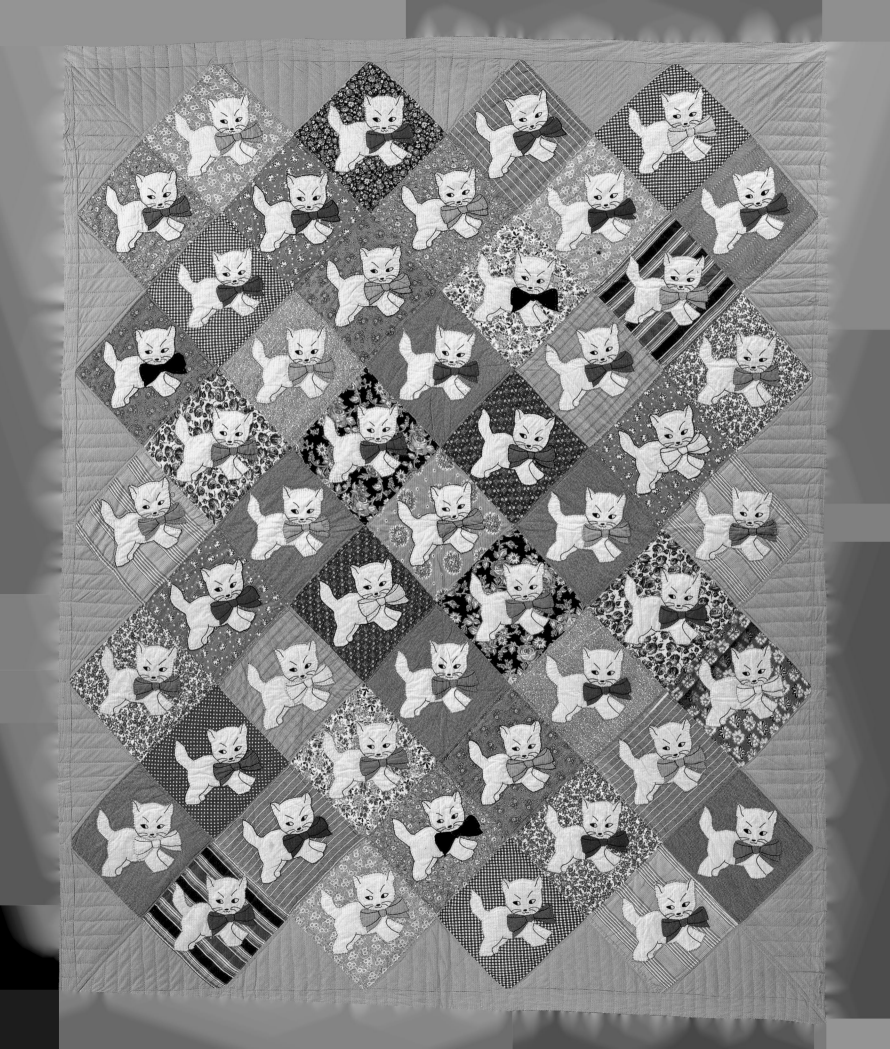

Compass and Wreath Quilt

Artist unidentified

Pennsylvania

1930–1935

Century of Progress Quilt

Artist unidentified

Ohio

Dated 1933

Double Wedding Ring Quilt

Artist unidentified

United States

1940–1950

Double Wedding Ring Quilt

Artist unidentified

Probably Georgia

1930–1940

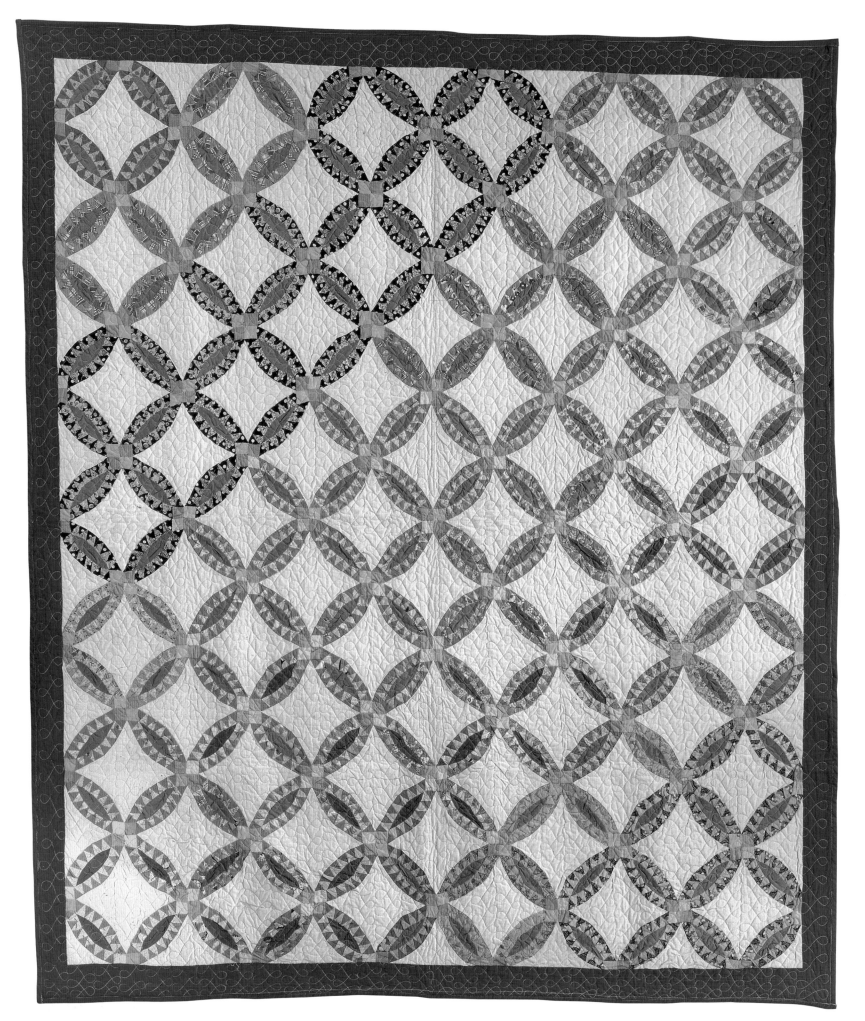

Indian Wedding Ring Quilt

Artist unidentified

United States

1935–1945

Golden Wedding Ring Quilt

Artist unidentified

United States

1934–1940

Friendship Knot Quilt

Artist unidentified

United States

1945–1960

Sampler Quilt

Artist unidentified

United States

1935–1945

Dresden Plate Quilt

Artist unidentified

United States

1930–1940

Tied Stars Quilt

Artist unidentified

United States

1900–1940

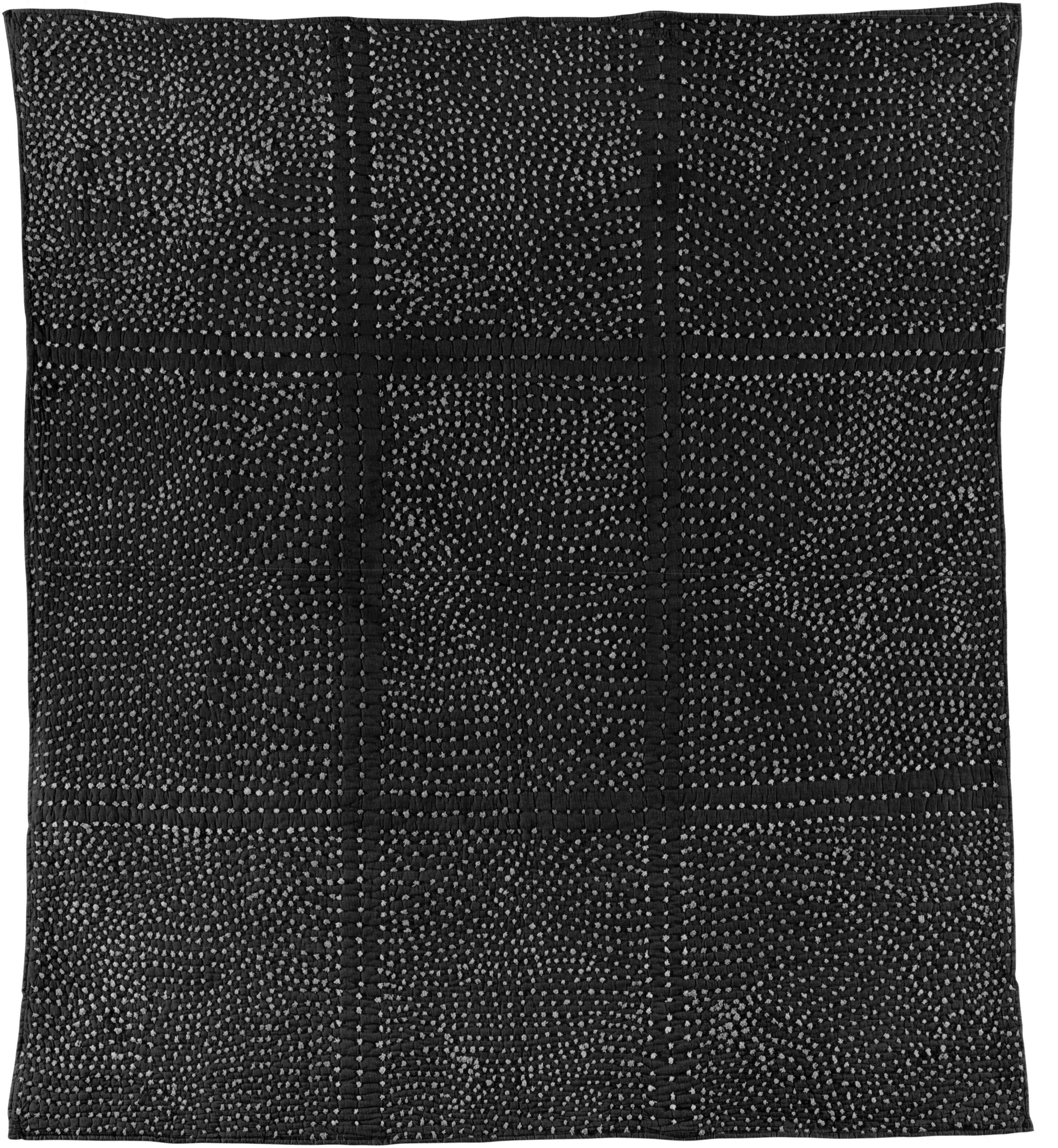

THE AMISH QUILT

The strong religious beliefs of the Amish and their desire to live apart from the outside world have influenced the distinctive appearance of their quilts. The Amish in America are descendants of the Swiss Brethren, who were part of the Anabaptist movement that followed the Reformation in the sixteenth century. Named for their founder, the conservative Swiss Mennonite elder Jakob Ammann (possibly 1644–before 1730), the Amish were harshly persecuted in Europe for their religious beliefs. At the invitation of William Penn, the founder of the Province of Pennsylvania and a staunch promoter of religious freedom, many of them immigrated to America, along with other Pennsylvania Germans, in the first quarter of the eighteenth century. During the Colonial period, they settled on the rich farmland of Berks, Chester, and Lancaster Counties in Pennsylvania, where they could continue to live the way of life they had led in Europe, and which they essentially lead today. By the nineteenth century, the Amish had also formed communities in western Pennsylvania (including Mifflin County) and a number of Midwestern states, such as Ohio, Indiana, and Illinois.

The Amish, like other Germanic groups, did not bring a tradition of quiltmaking to America with them. Blankets, featherbeds, and woven coverlets were the more typical style of bedding. The Amish learned to make quilts from their "English" neighbors (the name they gave all people outside their sect), but it was not until the late nineteenth century that the quiltmaking tradition truly took hold among Amish women.

As befits their makers' conservative lifestyle and religious prohibition against naturalistic images, Amish quilts are typically made of geometric pieces of solid-colored fabric. Patterned fabrics, although occasionally used in an inconspicuous way, are considered too "worldly" for quilt tops, and appliqués are deemed frivolous, decorative additions that are not functional. Lancaster County quilts (pages 242–247) are particularly renowned for their large geometric designs made in fine-quality, jewel-tone wools. Diamond in the Square, a pattern that originated in Lancaster County (pages 242 and 243), is actually an Amish adaptation of the center-medallion style of quilt popular among "English" quiltmakers in the first half of the nineteenth century (see, for example, page 53). The Amish women may have deliberately chosen patterns that were outmoded in the outside world in an attempt to make their quilts in accordance with Amish standards of nonconformity to English fashions.

Amish quilts made in Mifflin County, Pennsylvania, (pages 248–253) generally display a wider variety of patterns and fabrics than those made in Lancaster County, although there is a decided preference for a variety of four- and nine-patch designs. Even the *Crazy Patch Quilt* (page 252), obviously an Amish adaptation of a design popular in the outside world at an earlier time, can be viewed as a traditional Mifflin County four-patch.

By far the largest number of Amish quilts were made in the Midwest (pages 254–281), particularly Ohio and Indiana. This reflects the large settlements of Amish in these states, as well as the popularity of quiltmaking in the Amish communities. Perhaps the greatest difference between Amish quilts made in the Midwest and those made in Pennsylvania is the larger number of patterns found in the Midwest, both those borrowed from the outside world and those originated by the Amish. The greater variety of patterns may be a by-product of the fact that the Amish in Ohio, Indiana, Illinois, and elsewhere in the Midwest do not live in such concentrated communities as their counterparts in Pennsylvania and consequently have more opportunities to be exposed to the influences of world around them. Typically, the quilts are block designs surrounded, like most Amish quilts, by a narrow inner border and a wide outer border, and cotton is the preferred fabric.

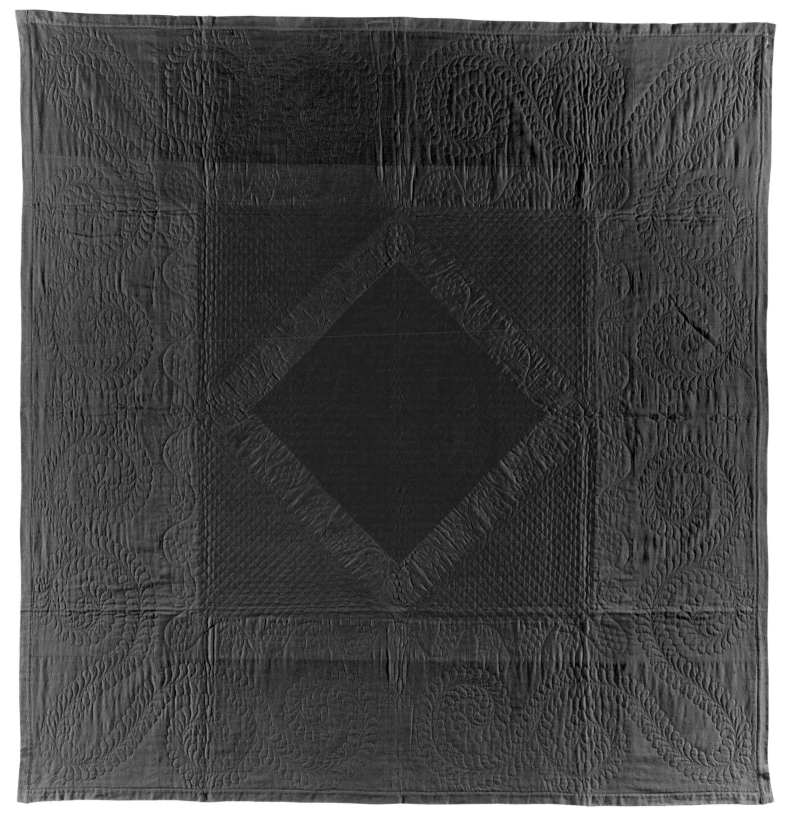

Diamond in the Square Quilt

Artist unidentified

Lancaster County, Pennsylvania

1910–1925

The Amish Quilt

Diamond in the Square Quilt

Artist unidentified

Lancaster County, Pennsylvania

1910–1930

Sawtooth Diamond in the Square Quilt

Artist unidentified

Lancaster County, Pennsylvania

1921–1935

Bars Quilt

Artist unidentified

Lancaster County, Pennsylvania

1910–1920

Double Nine-Patch Quilt

Artist unidentified

Lancaster County, Pennsylvania

1930–1940

Sunshine and Shadow Quilt

Artist unidentified

Lancaster County, Pennsylvania

1930–1940

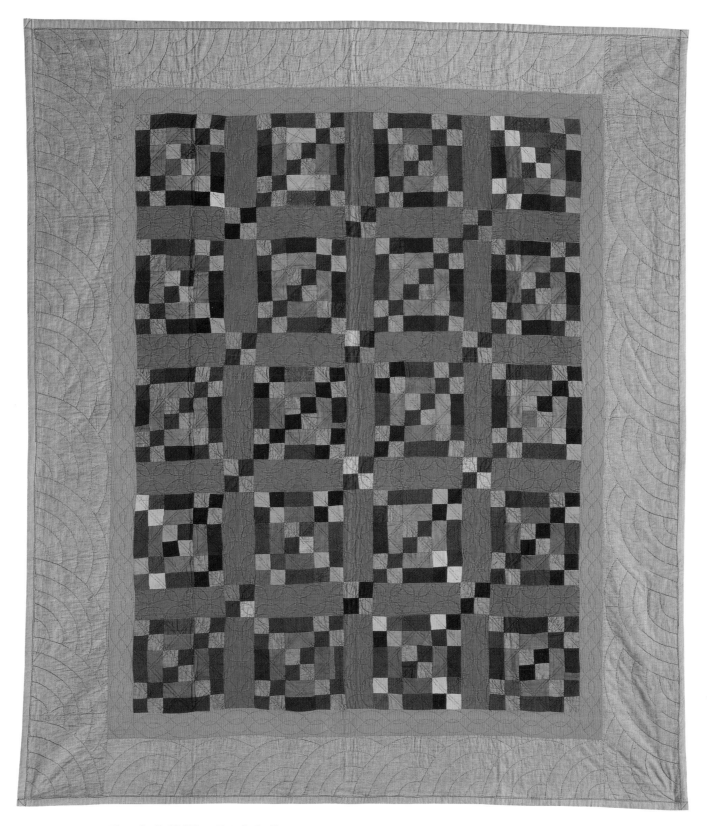

Four in Split Nine-Patch Quilt

Lydia A. (Yoder) Hostetler (dates unknown), embroidered "LAY"

Mifflin County, Pennsylvania, White Topper Amish

1920–1930

Four-Patch and Triangles Quilt

Barbara Zook Peachey (1848–1930)

Mifflin County, Pennsylvania, Yellow Topper Amish, Byler Group

1910–1920

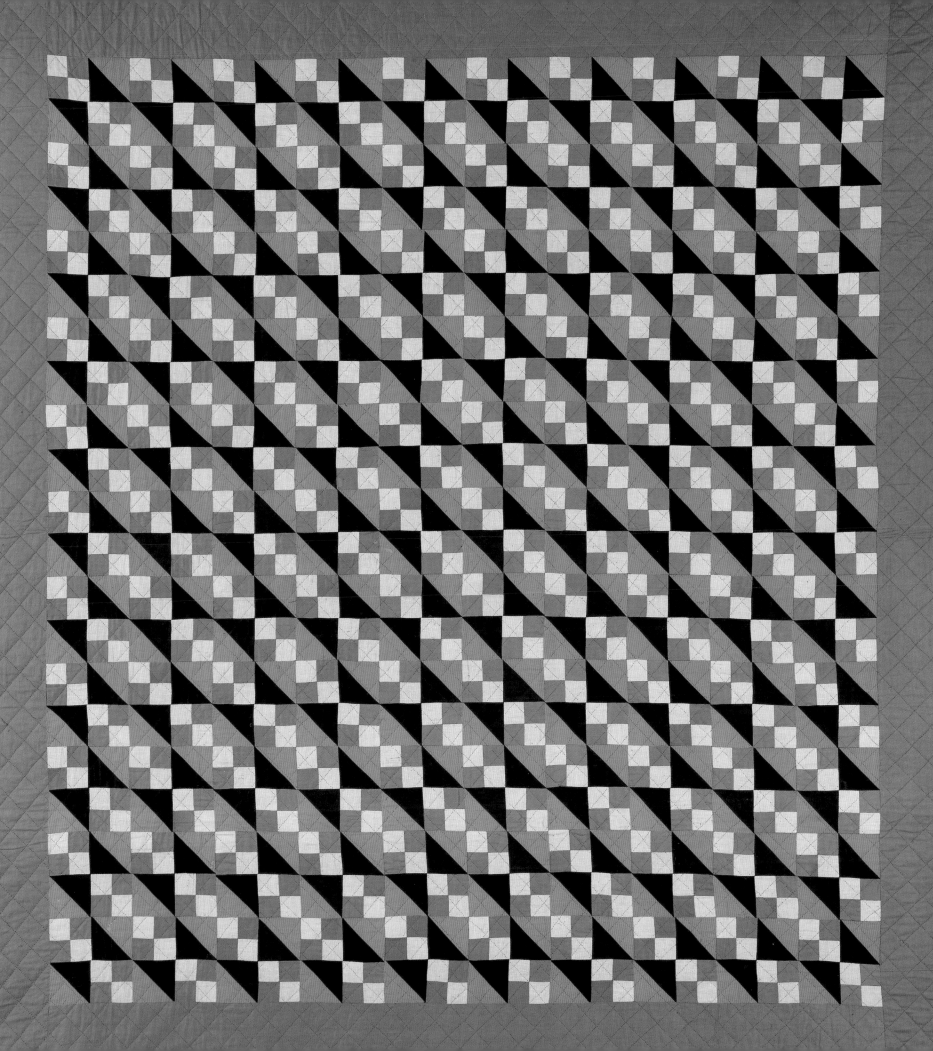

Four-Patch in Block-Work Quilt

Annie M. Peachey (Mrs. David M.) Swarey (1902–?)

Mifflin County, Pennsylvania, Yellow Topper Amish, Byler Group

1925–1935

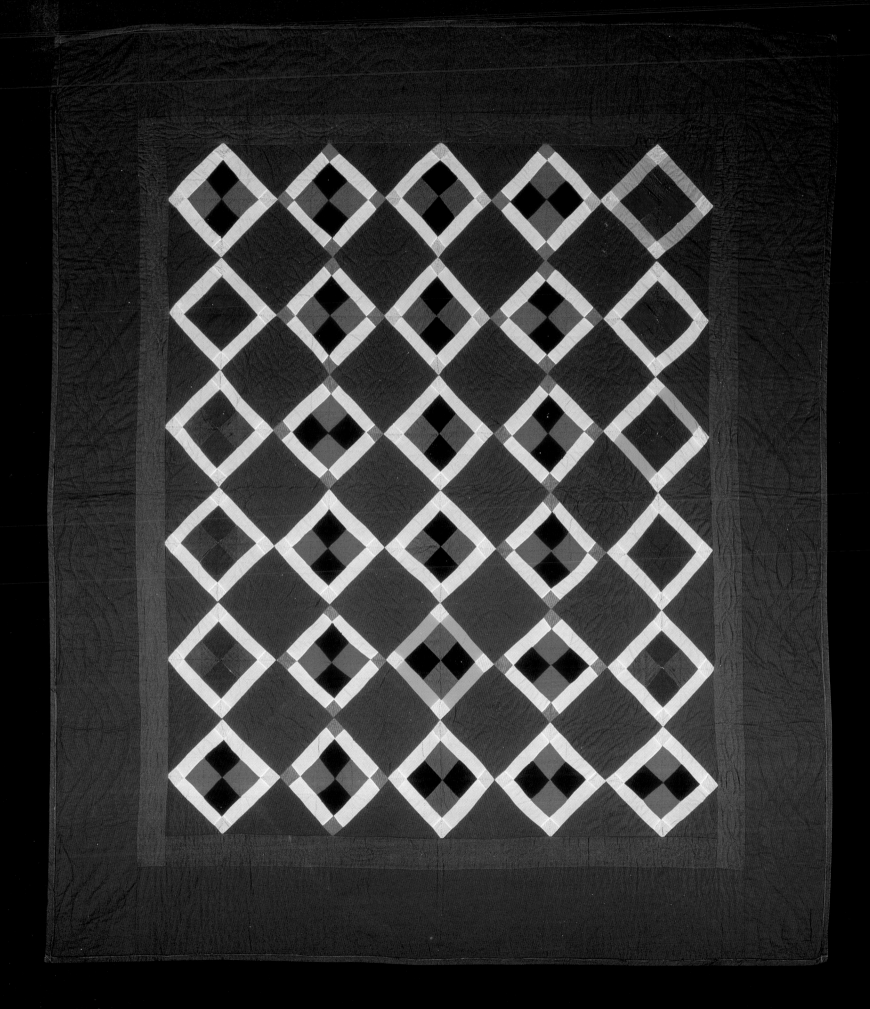

Log Cabin Quilt, Barn Raising Variation

Lydia A. (Kanagy) Peachey (1863–1949)

Mifflin County, Pennsylvania, Black Topper Amish, Peachey Group

1890–1900

Crazy Patch Quilt

Leah Zook Hartzler (dates unknown)

Mifflin County, Pennsylvania, Black Topper Amish, Peachey Group

Dated 1903

Inside Border Child's Quilt

Artist unidentified

Midwestern United States

1925–1935

Double Inside Border Quilt

Artist unidentified

Probably Ohio

1910–1925

254   **The Amish Quilt**

Center Star with Corner Stars Quilt

Unidentified member of the Glick Family

Probably Arthur, Illinois

1890–1900

One-Patch Quilt

Artist unidentified

Midwestern United States

Dated 1921

Double Nine-Patch Lounge Quilt

Mrs. Dan Troyer (dates unknown)

Holmes County, Ohio

1915–1925

Pinwheel and Nine-Patch Child's Quilt

Artist unidentified

Midwestern United States

1950–1960

Carpenter's Wheel Variation Quilt

Artist unidentified

Midwestern United States

1945–1955

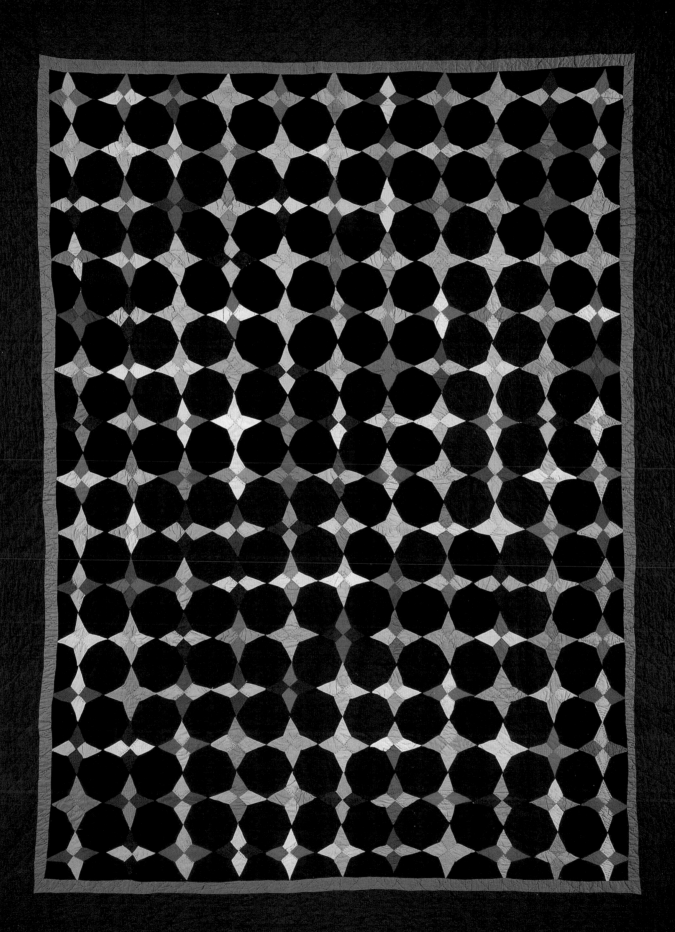

Hole in the Barn Door Variation Quilt

Mrs. Menno Yoder (dates unknown), initialed "LMY"

Emma, Indiana

Dated 1942

Double T Quilt

Artist unidentified

Ohio

1920–1940

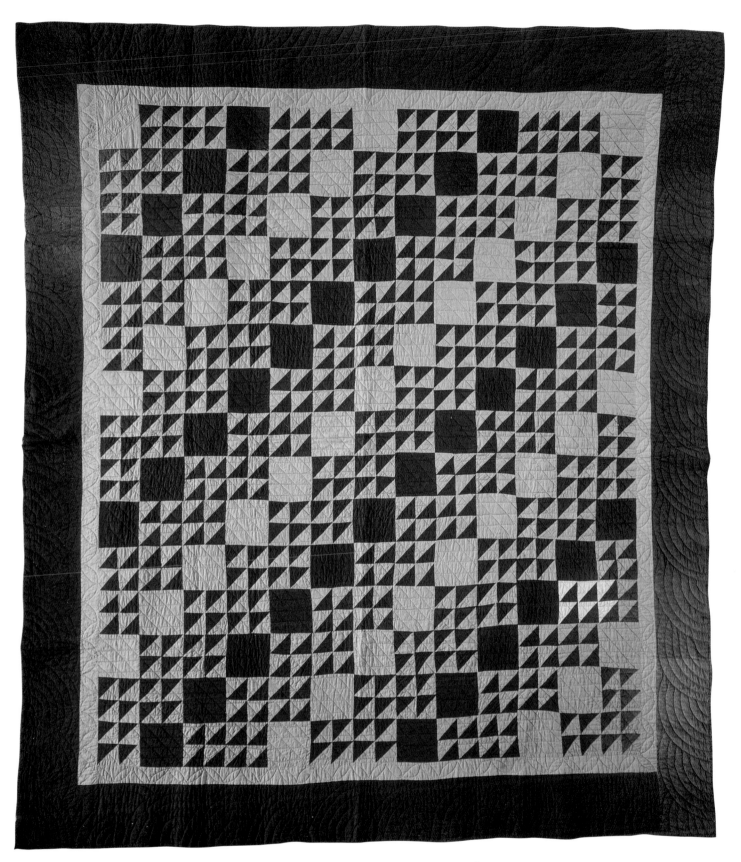

Ocean Waves Quilt

Anna Yoder Raber (dates unknown)

Honeyville, Indiana

1925–1935

Ocean Waves Variation Quilt

Artist unidentified

Emma, Indiana

1920–1930

Lone Star Quilt

Mrs. David Bontraeger (dates unknown), initialed "DB"

Emma, Indiana

1920–1930

Tumbling Blocks Quilt

Mrs. Ed Lantz (dates unknown)

Elkhart, Indiana

1910–1920

Variable Stars Crib Quilt

Artist unidentified

Midwestern United States

1960

Rolling Stone Quilt

Artist unidentified, initialed "LM"

Indiana

Dated 1925

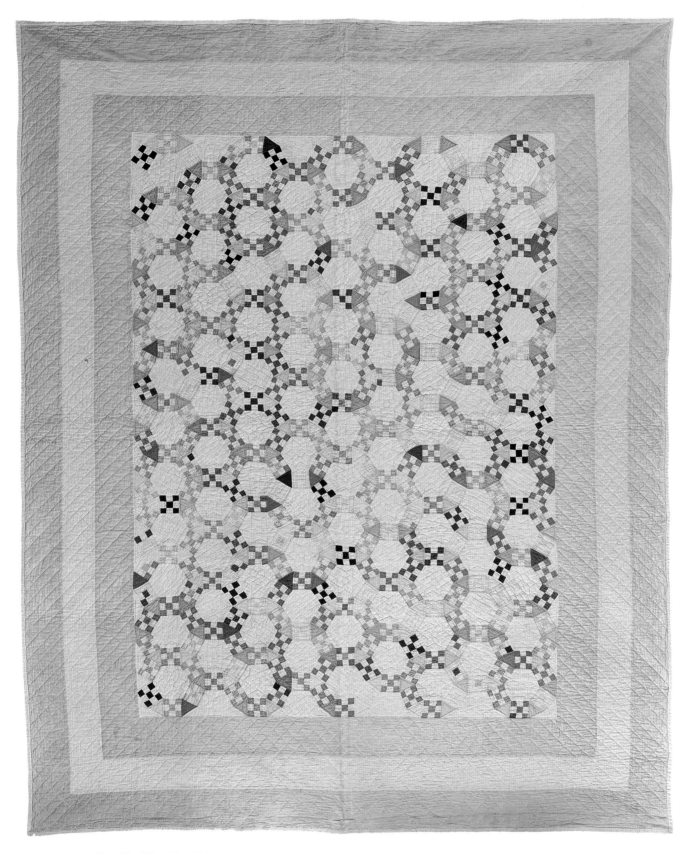

Double Wedding Ring Quilt

Susie (Mrs. Harry) Bontrager (?–1954)

Yoder, Kansas

1935–1945

Double Wedding Ring Quilt

Mrs. Andy G. Byler (dates unknown)

Atlantic, Pennsylvania

1930–1940

Fans Quilt

Artist unidentified, initialed "PM"

Indiana

1925–1935

Chinese Coins Quilt

Sarah Miller (dates unknown)

Haven, Kansas

1935

Trip Around the World Crib Quilt

Artist unidentified

Midwestern United States

1950–1960

Sailboats Quilt

Amanda Lehman (dates unknown)

Topeka, Indiana

1955–1965

The Amish Quilt

THE AFRICAN AMERICAN QUILT

The quilts illustrated in this chapter were made in the last quarter of the twentieth century by African American women in the rural South. With a few exceptions, they were acquired by the American Folk Art Museum in 1991 to fill a significant gap in the collection: quilts created within traditional African American communities by makers who shared similar backgrounds, artistic motivations, and aesthetics. Art historian Dr. Maude Southwell Wahlman, who examined and identified the quilts for the museum, argued that "most African American quiltmaking derives its aesthetic from various African traditions, both technological and ideological ones. Thus I deliberately study African American quilts which exhibit similar aesthetic tendencies with African textiles." However, Wahlman and other quilt historians agree that these quilts represent just a part of the story of African American quilts. As the late quilt historian Cuesta Benberry queried, "How could this small sample of late-twentieth-century African American quilts represent in its entirety the contributions of thousands of black quiltmakers working at the craft over two centuries?"

Wahlman identified seven traits that distinguish the African American quilts of the type shown here from the English American tradition: an emphasis on vertical strips, bright colors, large designs, asymmetry, improvisation, symbolic forms, and multiple patterning. Strip piecing, for example, seen particularly on Idabell Bester's *Strip Quilt* (page 284), is a primary construction technique seen in West African and Caribbean textiles. Large shapes and strong, contrasting colors, apparent in Nora McKeown Ezell's *Star Quilt* (page 285) and Mary Maxtion's *Snail Trail Quilt* (page 286), have been related to the communicative function of African fabrics. Asymmetry and improvisation, qualities also seen in the textile tradition of West Africa, where woven strips with patterns are often sewn together to make a larger unpredictable design, are characteristics of many of the quilts illustrated here, including Lucinda Toomer's *Le Moyne Star Variation Quilt* (page 288) and Lureca Outland's *Diamond Four-Patch in Cross Quilt* (page 290). The diamond motif on the *Diamond Four-Patch in Cross Quilt* can also be viewed as a symbolic form, seen in African American arts, gravestones, houses, and paintings and representing the four directions, or the four moments, of the Kongo sun: birth, life, death, and rebirth. Multiple patterning is especially obvious in Mary Maxtion's *Everybody Quilt* (page 287). In West Africa, multiple-patterned cloth is believed to communicate the prestige, power, and wealth of the owners who can both name the different patterns and afford to pay the master weavers to create them. It is also believed that the complex designs keep evil spirits away. Furthermore, improvisation and multiple patterning ensure that copying is almost impossible.

Pearlie Posey's *Hens Quilt* (page 297) displays most of these characteristics but distinguishes itself from the other African American quilts in the museum's collection in that the hen shapes were appliquéd onto the quilt top. Appliquéd African American quilts have often been compared to the appliqué tradition found in a number of African cultures, most notably the tapestries made by the Fon of West Africa.

The final textile illustrated in this section, Jessie B. Telfair's *Freedom Quilt* (page 299), one of forty-three quilts the artist created in this design, can be interpreted to have African influences, but Telfair gave it a very American meaning: according to the artist, she stitched these quilts to capture in cloth her feelings about having lost her job after she had tried to register to vote in the 1960s.

Strip Quilt

Idabell Bester (?–c. 1992), quilted by Losie Webb (dates unknown)

Alabama

Pieced 1980, quilted 1990

Star Quilt

Nora McKeown Ezell (1917–2007)

Eutaw, Alabama

Dated 1977

Snail Trail Quilt

Mary Maxtion (b. 1924)

Boligee, Alabama

1990

Everybody Quilt

Mary Maxtion (b. 1924)

Boligee, Alabama

1989

Le Moyne Star Variation Quilt

Lucinda Toomer (1888–1983)

Macon, Georgia

1981

Diamond Strip Quilt

Lucinda Toomer (1888–1983)

Macon, Georgia

c. 1975

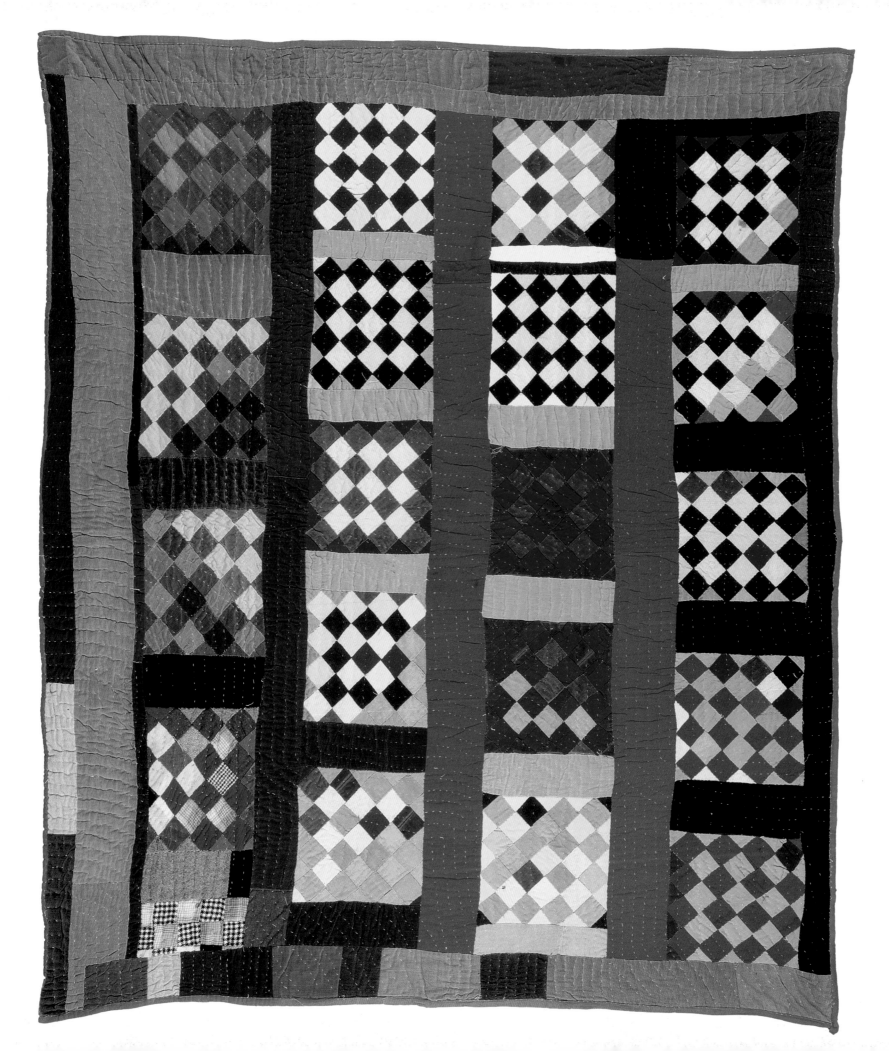

Diamond Four-Patch in Cross Quilt

Lureca Outland (c. 1904–2009)

Boligee, Alabama

1991

Wedding Ring Interpretation Quilt

Lureca Outland (c. 1904–2009)

Boligee, Alabama

1991

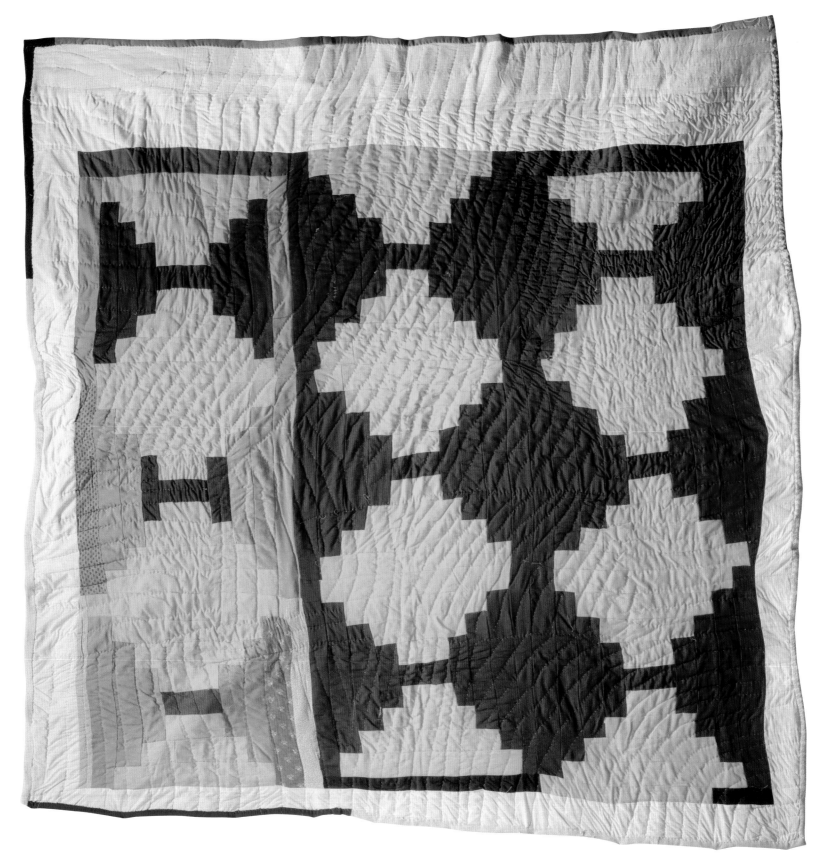

Pig Pen Quilt, Log Cabin Variation

Pecolia Warner (1901–1983)

Yazoo City, Mississippi

1982

Log Cabin Quilt, Courthouse Steps Variation

Plummer T. Pettway (1918–1993)

Boykin, Alabama

1991

Star of Bethlehem with Satellite Stars Quilt

Leola Pettway (b. 1929)

Boykin, Alabama

1991

Sailboats Quilt

Alean Pearson (b. 1918)

Oxford, Mississippi

1985

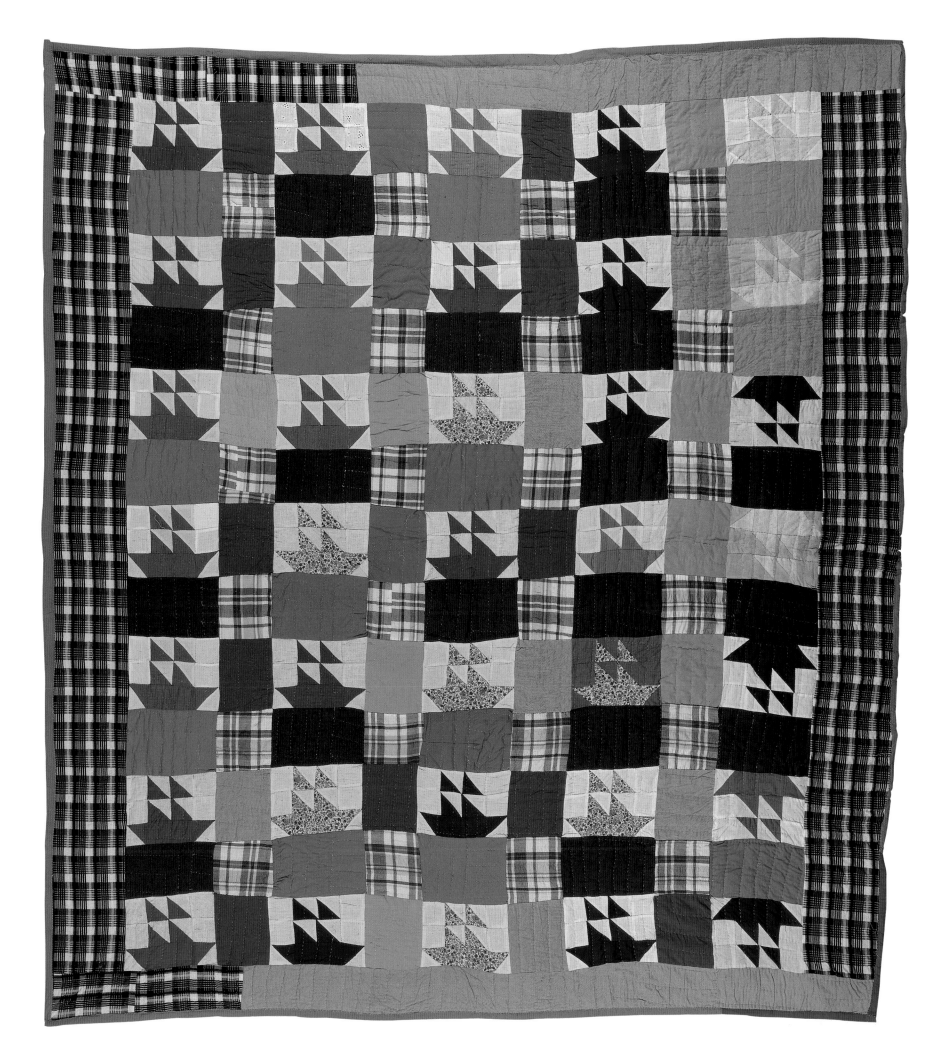

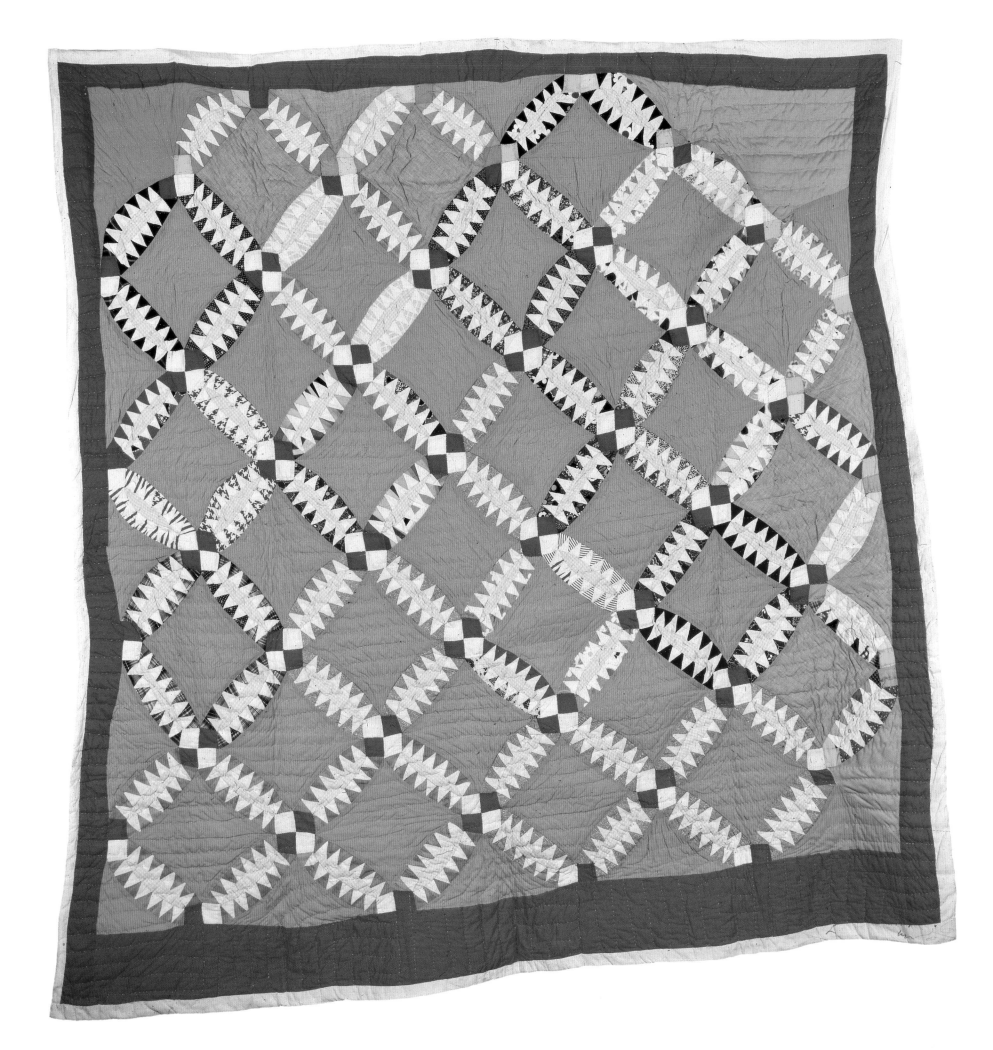

Rattlesnake Quilt

Alean Pearson (b. 1918)

Oxford, Mississippi

1985

Hens Quilt

Pearlie Posey (1894–1984)

Yazoo City, Mississippi

1981

Freedom Quilt

Jessie B. Telfair (1913–1986)

Parrott, Georgia

Dated 1983

FREEDOM
FREEDOM
FREEDOM
FREEDOM
FREEDOM
FREEDOM
FREEDOM

THE CONTEMPORARY QUILT

A variety of influences contributed to a resurgence of quiltmaking in America and around the world beginning in the mid-twentieth century: the crafts revival of the 1960s, a nostalgia craze and revived appreciation of American arts and antiques (and especially quilts) that was encouraged by a number of museum exhibitions in the early 1970s, and the nation's bicentennial celebrations in 1976, which aroused interest in the artistic traditions of America's past much as the centennial celebrations had a hundred years earlier. Women and men, hobbyists and professional needleworkers joined in a reinvigoration of quiltmaking that continues unabated to this day. As the examples shown on the following pages indicate, however, quilts made in the late twentieth and early twenty-first centuries are often very different from those made by prior generations.

Although quilts are still created for use on a bed, there is an increased likelihood today that a quilt (and the term is often loosely used for various three-layered works of art) will be made specifically for display on a wall. Makers of the works illustrated here are often referred to as "fiber artists," and while some use techniques that have been honed by quiltmakers for generations, often their art expands the boundaries of traditional quiltmaking in terms of materials, sewing, size, and shape.

Hystercine Rankin came to quiltmaking from a traditional background and used more conventional materials for her work of textile art (page 313). She began making quilts when she was 12 years old to help keep her ten brothers and sister warm. Rankin continued this work for her own family, providing quilts for each of her seven children. Over the years, she has passed her knowledge on to many children in her community, a continuity of tradition that typifies more than three hundred years of American quiltmaking. Most recently, she has been making "memory quilts" such as the example shown here, using appliqué and embroidery to create works of textile art that relate family stories and scenes from her life.

Paula Nadelstern is renowned in the contemporary quilt world for works such as *Kaleidoscopic XVI: More Is More* (page 315) but says she does not make quilts because she loves kaleidoscopes, she makes them because she loves printed textiles. Early in her career as a quilt artist, Nadelstern was inspired by a bolt of sensuous and beautiful Liberty of London fabric. The bilateral symmetry of the design was an epiphany that stirred her imagination, yielding a seemingly infinite vein of creative expression for more than twenty years.

As in generations past, quiltmaking is often a group activity—quilt guilds and organizations around the world meet for many of the same reasons for which quiltmakers have always gathered. The *National Tribute* *Quilt* (pages 316–317), permanently on display in the museum's Lincoln Square branch, represents the response of the Steel Quilters of the United States Steel Corporation to the events of September 11, 2001. This small quilt club conceived the monumental undertaking, ultimately receiving quilt blocks from all fifty states as well as a number of countries overseas. The quilt measures eight feet high by thirty feet wide and is constructed of 3,466 blocks in six panels. Each three-inch-square block bears the name of one person who perished in the attacks.

Polynesia, the Sky

Fran Soika (b. c. 1924)

Novelty, Ohio

Dated 1981

Detail of quilt back

Reflection

Kathyanne White (b. 1950)

Prescott, Arizona

2001

Bittersweet XII

Nancy Crow (b. 1943), quilted by Velma Brill (dates unknown)

Baltimore, Ohio, and Cambridge, Ohio

1980

Stars over Hawaii Quilt

Mary K. Borkowski (1916–2008)

Dayton, Ohio

1979

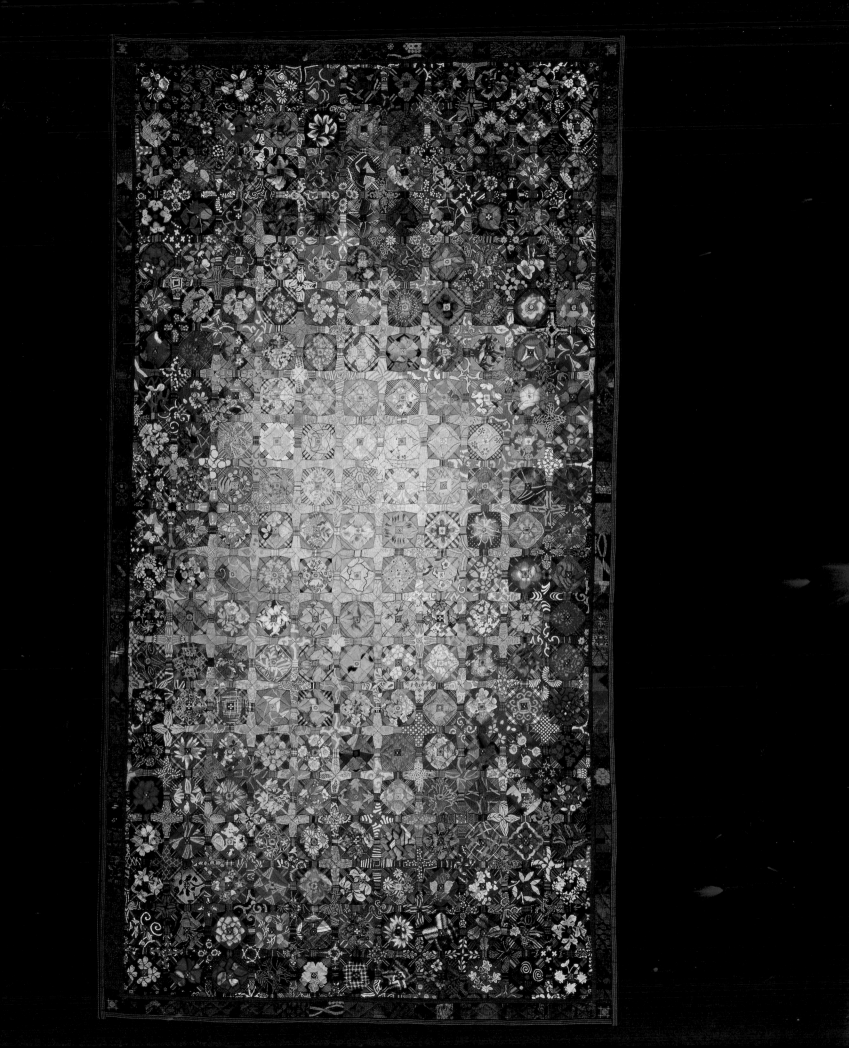

Kimono Hanging

Kumiko Sudo (dates unknown)

Berkeley, California

1988

Yuen no Akari: **Light from Far-Away Space**

Setsuko Obi (b. 1942)

Tokyo, Japan

2001

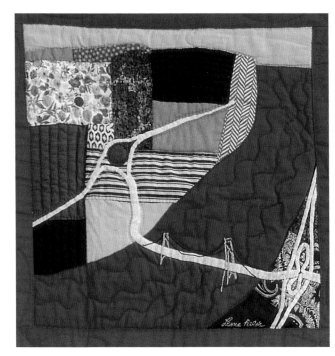

Hudson River Quilt

Irene Preston Miller (1917–2007) and the Hudson River Quilters

Croton-on-Hudson, New York

1969–1972

Untitled Family History Quilt

Hystercine Rankin (b. 1929)

Port Gibson, Mississippi

1990–2000

Kaleidoscopic XVI: More Is More

Paula Nadelstern (b. 1951)

Bronx, New York

Dated 1996

National Tribute Quilt

Organized and assembled by the Steel Quilters

Pittsburgh

2002

Illustrations

THE WHOLE-CLOTH QUILT
Wool Whole-Cloth Quilts

Page 23
Indigo Calimanco Quilt
Artist unidentified
Probably New England
1800–1820
Glazed wool, 86 x 95"
Gift of Cyril Irwin Nelson in honor of Joel and Kate Kopp, 1999.20.1

Page 25
Calimanco Quilt
Artist unidentified
Possibly Philadelphia
1800–1825
Glazed wool, 100 x 96"
Gift of Cyril Irwin Nelson, 2005.11.26

Page 26
Harlequin Medallion Quilt
Artist unidentified
New England
1800–1820
Glazed wool, 87 x 96"
Gift of Cyril Irwin Nelson in loving memory of his grandparents John Williams and Sophie Anna Macy, 1984.33.1

Page 27
Center Star Quilt
Artist unidentified
New England
1815–1825
Glazed wool, 100½ x 98"
Gift of Cyril Irwin Nelson in honor of Robert Bishop, American Folk Art Museum director (1977–1991), 1986.13.1

Page 28
Pieced Quilt
Artist unidentified
New England
1810–1820
Wool, 96 x 88"
Gift of Cyril Irwin Nelson, 2005.11.4

Page 29
Pieced Quilt
Artist unidentified
Probably New England
1820–1840
Wool, 92 x 84½"
Gift of Cyril Irwin Nelson, 2005.11.11

Chintz and Copperplate-Printed Whole-Cloth Quilts

Page 30
Chintz Whole-Cloth Quilt
Artist unidentified
Probably United States
1810–1820
Cotton, 91¼ x 87"
Gift of Cyril Irwin Nelson in honor of Joel and Kate Kopp, 1993.6.7

Page 31
Chintz Whole-Cloth Quilt
Artist unidentified
Probably United States
1830–1840
Cotton, 96½ x 90"
Gift of Cyril Irwin Nelson, 1999.20.2

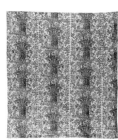

Page 32
Pillar-Print Whole-Cloth Quilt
Artist unidentified
United States
1825–1835
Cotton, 87 x 78"
Gift of Cyril Irwin Nelson, 2005.11.29

Page 33
Copperplate-Printed Whole-Cloth Quilt
Artist unidentified
Probably England
1785–1790
Linen and cotton, 96 x 93"
Gift of Cyril Irwin Nelson in honor of Laura Fisher, 1995.13.3

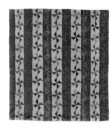

THE SIGNATURE QUILT
Friendship Quilts

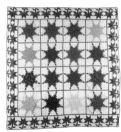
Album Quilts

Page 73

Baltimore-Style Album Quilt Top

Artist unidentified

Baltimore; found in Uniontown, Pennsylvania

1845–1850

Cotton with wool embroidery, 84 x 82"

Gift of Altria Group, Inc., 2008.9.3

Page 75

Reiter Family Album Quilt

Artist unidentified, descended in the family of Katie Friedman Reiter (1873–1942) and Liebe Gross Friedman (dates unknown)

Probably Baltimore

1848–1850

Cotton and wool, 101 x 101"

Gift of Katherine Amelia Wine in honor of her grandmother Theresa Reiter Gross and the makers of the quilt, her great-grandmother Katie Friedman Reiter and her great-great-grandmother Liebe Gross Friedman, and on behalf of a generation of cousins: Sydney Howard Reiter, Penelope Breyer Tarplin, Jonnie Breyer Stahl, Susan Reiter Blinn, Benjamin Joseph Gross, and Leba Gross Wine, 2000.2.1

Page 77

Album Quilt

Possibly Sarah Morrell (dates unknown) and others

Pennsylvania and New Jersey

Dated 1843

Cotton and ink with cotton embroidery, 93¼ x 95¼"

Gift of Jeremy L. Banta, 1986.16.1

Page 78

Dunn Album Quilt

Sewing Society of the Fulton Street United Methodist Episcopal Church

Elizabethport, New Jersey

Dated 1852

Cotton and ink with cotton embroidery, 100 x 99¼"

Gift of Phyllis Haders, 1980.1.1

Page 81

Presentation Quilt for William A. Sargent

Members of the Freewill Baptist Church

Loudon, New Hampshire

Blocks made c. 1854, assembled and quilted later

Cotton with ink and cotton embroidery, 81 x 79"

Gift of Cyril Irwin Nelson, 2003.1.1

Page 83

Cross River Album Quilt

Mrs. Eldad Miller (1805–1874) and others

Cross River, New York

Dated 1861

Cotton and silk with wool embroidery, 90 x 75"

Gift of Dr. Stanley and Jacqueline Schneider, 1980.8.1

Page 84

Schoolhouse Quilt Top

The Presbyterian Ladies of Oak Ridge, Missouri

Oak Ridge, Missouri

1897–1898

Cotton with cotton embroidery, 74½ x 90½"

Gift of Beverly Walker Reitz in memory of Vest Walker, 1984.22.10

Page 87

Admiral Dewey Commemorative Quilt

Possibly the Mite Society (Ladies' Aid), United Brethren Church

Center Point, Indiana

1900–1910

Cotton with Turkey red cotton embroidery, 88 x 65"

Gift of Janet Gilbert for Marie Griffin, 1993.3.1

Page 89

McKinley Community Church Signature Quilt

Ladies' Aid Society, McKinley Community Church

Warren, Ohio

Dated 1935

Wool with wool yarn and embroidery thread, 86 x 74½"

Gift of Ivan Massar, 2007.2.1

THE APPLIQUÉ QUILT

Floral Appliqué Quilts

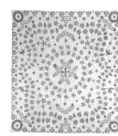

Page 92

Turkey Tracks Quilt

Artist unidentified

Possibly Ohio

1840–1850

Cotton, 90 x 86"

Gift of Cyril Irwin Nelson in honor of Laura Fisher, 1998.13.1

Page 93

"MTD" Quilt Top

Artist unidentified, appliquéd initials "MTD"

United States

Dated 1842

Cotton, 99 x 94"

Gift of Cyril Irwin Nelson, 2005.9.1

Page 95

Strawberries in Pots Quilt

Artist unidentified

Possibly Missouri

1850–1860

Cotton, 91 x 89"

Gift of Phyllis Haders, 1981.18.1

Page 97
Hearts and Pineapples Quilt Top
Artist unidentified
Probably Pennsylvania
1850–1870
Cotton, 87 x 69½"
Gift of Cyril Irwin Nelson in memory of his grandparents Guerdon Stearns and Elinor Irwin
(Chase) Holden, and in honor of his parents, Cyril Arthur and Elise Macy Nelson, 1982.22.4

Page 98
Floral Crib Quilt
Artist unidentified
United States
1850–1880
Cotton, 46 x 39"
Gift of Cyril Irwin Nelson, 1998.13.2

Page 99
Whig Rose Quilt
Abigail Hill (dates unknown)
Probably Indiana
Dated 1857–1858
Cotton, 79¾ x 70"
Gift of Irene Reichert in honor of her daughter, Susan Reichert Sink, and granddaughter,
Heather Sink, 1992.13.1

Page 100
Whig Rose Quilt with Swag and Tassel Border
Artist unidentified
United States
1850–1860
Cotton, 100 x 82"
Gift of Irene Reichert in honor of Nathan Druet, 1993.1.2

Page 101
Whig Rose Quilt
Artist unidentified
Possibly Pennsylvania
1860–1880
Cotton, 96¼ x 94¼"
Gift of Karen and Werner Gundersheimer, 1980.20.1

Page 102
Sunflowers Quilt
Artist unidentified
Possibly Pennsylvania
1860–1880
Cotton, 82 x 66½"
Gift of Cyril Irwin Nelson in honor of Laura Fisher, 2003.9.1

Page 103
Sunflowers and Hearts Quilt
Artist unidentified
Possibly New England
1860–1880
Cotton, 85 x 91"
Gift of Frances and Paul Martinson, 1994.2.1

Page 105
Oak Leaves with Cherries Quilt
Artist unidentified
United States
1870–1880
Cotton with wool embroidery, 80 x 78"
Gift of Irene Reichert, 1993.1.1

Page 107
Floral Medallion Quilt
Artist unidentified
Possibly Vincennes, Indiana
1870–1880
Cotton, 86 x 70"
Gift of Irene Reichert, 1993.1.3

Page 109
Centennial Quilt
Possibly Gertrude Knappenberger (dates unknown)
Possibly Emmaus, Pennsylvania
Dated 1876
Cotton with cotton embroidery, 82½ x 74½"
Gift of Rhea Goodman, 1979.9.1

Sampler Appliqué Quilts

Page 110
Patterns for Bird of Paradise Quilt Top
Artist unidentified
Vicinity of Albany, New York
1858–1863
Pencil on newspaper, 4" to 10¾" high
Gift of the Trustees of the American Folk Art Museum, 1979.7.2a–k

Page 111
Bird of Paradise Quilt Top
Artist unidentified
Vicinity of Albany, New York
1858–1863
Cotton, wool, and silk with ink and silk embroidery, 84½ x 69⅝"
Gift of the Trustees of the American Folk Art Museum, 1979.7.1

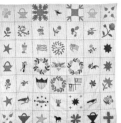

Pictorial Appliqué Quilts

Miscellaneous Appliqué Quilts

THE PIECED QUILT
Geometric Quilts

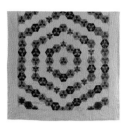

Page 132
Pennsylvania Hex Quilt
Artist unidentified
United States
1860–1900
Cotton, 94 x 100"
Gift of David L. Davies, 1997.4.2

Page 133
Stars Quilt
Unidentified member of the Hemiup Family
Geneva, New York
1860–1900
Cotton, 88½ x 80½"
Gift of Louise Emerson Francke, 1996.8.1

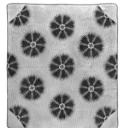

Page 135
Slashed Star Quilt
Sara Maartz (dates unknown)
Lancaster, Pennsylvania
Dated 1872
Cotton, 82 x 76"
Gift of Mr. and Mrs. Alan Weinstein, 2007.15.1

Page 136
Indian Pine Quilt
Artist unidentified, embroidered initials "BB"
Maine
1880–1890
Cotton with cotton embroidery, 86 x 82"
Gift of Cyril Irwin Nelson in memory of his grandparents Guerdon Stearns and Elinor Irwin
(Chase) Holden, and in honor of his parents, Cyril Arthur and Elise Macy Nelson, 1982.22.1

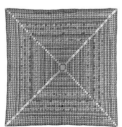

Page 137
Triangles and Flying Geese Quilt
Artist unidentified
United States
1875–1900
Cotton, 83 x 78"
Gift of Leo Rabkin, 2008.20.1

Page 138
Double T Quilt
Artist unidentified
Possibly New York State, Pennsylvania, or Ontario
1880–1900
Wool, 74 x 56"
Gift of Mr. and Mrs. Alan Weinstein, 2007.15.4

Page 139
Cross and Block Quilt
Artist unidentified
Possibly New York State, Pennsylvania, or Ontario
1880–1900
Wool, 71 x 76"
Gift of Mr. and Mrs. Alan Weinstein, 2007.15.5

Page 141
Four-Patch Quilt
Artist unidentified
United States
1880–1900
Cotton, 81½ x 69"
Gift in memory of Cyril Irwin Nelson by Anna Nelson, 2007.12.2

Page 143
Diamonds Quilt
Artist unidentified
Possibly New York State, Pennsylvania, or Ontario
1880–1910
Wool, 66½ x 60"
Gift of Mr. and Mrs. Alan Weinstein, 2007.15.3

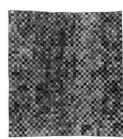

Page 144
Charm Quilt
Artist unidentified
United States
1880–1920
Cotton, 80 x 75½"
Gift of Freyda Rothstein, 1998.8.5

Page 145
Roman Cross Quilt
Artist unidentified
United States
1900–1920
Shirting cotton, 84½ x 82½"
Gift of Cyril Irwin Nelson, 2005.11.19

Page 146
Ohio Star Crib Quilt
Artist unidentified
United States
1920–1940
Cotton, 31½ x 30"
Gift of Frances Rasmussen in memory of her daughter, Cathyann, 2001.5.13

Commemorative and Pictorial Quilts

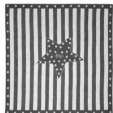

THE LOG CABIN QUILT
Log Cabin Quilts

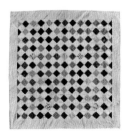

Page 164
Log Cabin Quilt, Courthouse Steps Variation
Artist unidentified
Possibly New York State
1880–1900
Silks, including satin, 75¾ x 64"
Gift of Mr. and Mrs. Alan Weinstein, 2007.15.7

Page 166
Log Cabin Crib Quilt, Courthouse Steps Variation
Artist unidentified
United States
1920–1950
Cotton, 46 x 33½"
Gift of Cyril Irwin Nelson, 1998.13.4

Page 167
Log Cabin Quilt, Courthouse Steps Variation
Samuel Steinberger (1865–c. 1934)
New York City
1890–1910
Silk, 69½ x 58" (framed)
Gift of Cyril Irwin Nelson in honor of Robert Bishop, American Folk Art Museum director (1977–1991), 1990.17.8

Page 169
Log Cabin Quilt, Windmill Blades Variation
Ada Hapman (Mrs. William) Kingsley (c. 1859–1939)
South Windsor, New York, or Athens, Pennsylvania
1880–1900
Silk, 73 x 65" (framed)
Gift of Margaret Cavigga, 1985.23.6

Page 171
Log Cabin Quilt, Pineapple Variation
Artist unidentified
Possibly Lancaster County, Pennsylvania
1880–1900
Cotton, 83¼ x 83"
Gift of Kinuko Fujii, 1991.8.1

Page 173
Log Cabin Quilt, Windmill Blades Variation
Artist unidentified
United States
1885–1920
Cotton, wool, and silks, including satin and velvet, 80 x 70"
Gift of Frances Rasmussen in memory of her daughter, Cathyann, 2001.5.21

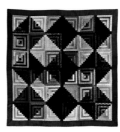

Page 175
Log Cabin Throw, Light-and-Dark Variation
Harriet Rutter Eagleson (1855–c. 1925)
New York City
1874–1880
Silk and cotton, 57¾ x 57¾"
Gift of Miss Jessica R. Eagleson, 1979.18.1

String Quilts

Page 176
String Quilt
Artist unidentified
Possibly Kentucky
1920–1940
Wool with cotton binding, 75¼ x 65"
Gift of Jolie Kelter and Michael Malcé, 1988.26.1

THE SHOW QUILT
Show Quilts

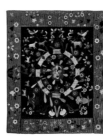

Page 180
Appliquéd and Embroidered Pictorial Bedcover
Artist unidentified
Possibly New York State
1825–1845
Wool, silk, cotton, and beads with silk and cotton embroidery, 87 x 86"
Gift of Ralph Esmerian, 1991.27.1

Page 181
Star of Bethlehem Quilt
Artist unidentified
Possibly Sullivan County, New York
1880–1900
Silk, 99 x 94¼"
Museum purchase made possible with funds from the Great American Quilt Festival 2, 1990.15.1

Page 183
Soldier's Quilt
Artist unidentified
Probably United States, Canada, or Great Britain
1854–1890
Wool melton, 67 x 66½"
Gift of Altria Group, Inc., 2008.9.1

Page 184
Variable Stars Quilt
Artist unidentified
United States
1880–1900
Silk, 94 x 78"
Gift of Anna Nelson in honor of Cyril Irwin Nelson's many contributions to
the American Folk Art Museum, 2007.12.4

Page 185
Oregon Pioneer Organization Quilt for Euda Aletha Kelly
Eudoxia Aurora Kelly Niblin (1865–1945)
Oregon
Dated 1923
Silk with silk embroidery, 73 x 67¾" (framed)
Gift of Margaret Cavigga, 1985.23.9

Page 186
Stars and Pentagons Quilt
Artist unidentified
United States
1880–1900
Silk, 81 x 44" (framed)
Gift of Jacqueline L. Fowler, 1981.2.1

Page 187
Show Quilt with Contained Crazy Stars
Unidentified member of the McAllister Family
Barnstead, New Hampshire
1885–1920
Silks, including satin, 55 x 54½"
Gift of Eleanor Knapp, 2007.9.1

Page 189
Map Quilt
Artist unidentified
Possibly Virginia
1886
Silk and cotton with silk embroidery, 78¾ x 82¼"
Gift of Dr. and Mrs. C. David McLaughlin, 1987.1.1

Crazy Quilts

Page 190
Crazy Quilt Top
Angelina Grattan (dates unknown)
United States
1880–1890
Silks, including velvets, satins, and brocades, with embroidery, 77 x 76"
Gift of Elizabeth B. Dichman Smith, 2004.19.1

Page 191
Center Star Crazy Throw
Mary Ann Crocker Hinman (1817–1893)
New York State
1880–1890
Silk with silk embroidery, 64 x 52¾"
Gift of Ruth E. Avard, 1993.2.1

Page 192
Equestrian Crazy Quilt
Artist unidentified
Possibly New York State
1880–1900
Silks, including velvet, and cotton with cotton embroidery, 92 x 61½"
Gift of Mr. and Mrs. James D. Clokey III, 1986.12.1

Page 193
Cleveland-Hendricks Crazy Quilt
Artist unidentified, initialed "J.F.R."
United States
1885–1890
Lithographed silk ribbons, silk, and wool with cotton fringe and silk and
metallic embroidery, 75 x 77"
Gift of Margaret Cavigga, 1985.23.3

Page 194
Crazy Quilt
Rachel Blair Greene (1846–1909)
Belvedere, New Jersey
1885–1895
Silk and paint with metallic and silk embroidery, 72 x 71¾"
Gift of James I. Chesterley, 1982.18.1

Page 196
"S.H." Crazy Quilt
Artist unidentified, initialed "S.H."
United States
1885–1895
Silk, ink, paint, and cotton with silk embroidery, 75 x 74"
Gift of Margaret Cavigga, 1985.23.4

Page 199
"Ella" Crazy Quilt
Artist unidentified, embroidered "Ella"
United States
Dated 1922
Suiting woolens with cotton floss embroidery, 84 x 68"
Gift of Frances S. Martinson, 2006.4.1

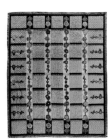

Page 222
English Flower Garden Quilt
Jennie Pingrey (Mrs. Charles O.) Stotts (c. 1861–?)
Yates Center, Kansas
1930–1935
Cotton, 95 x 77¾"
Gift of Cyril Irwin Nelson, 1987.17.1

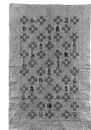

Page 223
Embroidered Floral Appliqué Quilt
Artist unidentified
United States
1930–1940
Cotton with cotton embroidery, 81 x 81"
Gift of Cyril Irwin Nelson in honor of Thos. K. Woodard
and Blanche Greenstein, 1993.6.4

Page 224
Outline Embroidered Child's Quilt
Artist unidentified
United States
Dated 1933
Cotton, 53½ x 36"
Gift of Cyril Irwin Nelson, 1993.6.3

Page 226
Gingham Dog and Calico Cat Crib Quilt
Artist unidentified
Probably Pennsylvania
1920–1930
Cotton, 33½ x 27½"
Gift of Gloria List, 1979.35.1

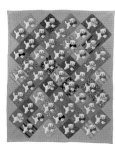

Page 227
Kitten Appliqué Quilt
Artist unidentified
Possibly Kentucky
1941–1950
Cotton, including muslin feed sacks, with cotton embroidery, 83 x 67"
Gift of Laura Fisher, Antique Quilts and Americana, 1987.8.1

Page 229
Star of France Quilt
Artist unidentified
United States
1930–1940
Cotton, 81¾ x 81¾"
Gift of Cyril Irwin Nelson in honor of Robert Bishop, American Folk Art Museum
director (1977–1991), 1990.17.4

Page 230
Compass and Wreath Quilt
Artist unidentified
Pennsylvania
1930–1935
Cotton with cotton embroidery, 88¾ x 78½"
Gift of Shelly Zegart, 1994.12.2

Page 231
Century of Progress Quilt
Artist unidentified
Ohio
Dated 1933
Cotton with cotton embroidery, 88½ x 74¼"
Gift of Shelly Zegart, 1995.26.1

Page 232
Double Wedding Ring Quilt
Artist unidentified
United States
1940–1950
Cotton and muslin, 82 x 81"
Gift of Robert Bishop, 1993.4.14

Page 233
Double Wedding Ring Quilt
Artist unidentified
Probably Georgia
1930–1940
Cotton, 86¼ x 72" (framed)
Gift of Robert Bishop, 1993.4.19

Page 234
Indian Wedding Ring Quilt
Artist unidentified
United States
1935–1945
Cotton, 82½ x 70¾" (framed)
Gift of Robert Bishop, 1993.4.38

Page 235
Golden Wedding Ring Quilt
Artist unidentified
United States
1934–1940
Cotton, 81¼ x 72½" (framed)
Gift of Robert Bishop, 1993.4.3

Page 236
Friendship Knot Quilt
Artist unidentified
United States
1945–1960
Cotton and cotton blends, 87 x 75½"
Gift of Robert Bishop, 1990.25.19

Page 237
Sampler Quilt
Artist unidentified
United States
1935–1945
Cotton, 84 x 71¾" (framed)
Gift of Robert Bishop, 1993.4.8

Page 238
Dresden Plate Quilt
Artist unidentified
United States
1930–1940
Cotton, 84 x 66"
Gift of Cyril Irwin Nelson, 2005.11.17

Page 239
Tied Stars Quilt
Artist unidentified
United States
1900–1940
Cotton with cotton and wool embroidery, 76 x 71"
Gift of Mary and Al Shands, 2008.8.1

THE AMISH QUILT
Lancaster County Quilts

Page 242
Diamond in the Square Quilt
Artist unidentified
Lancaster County, Pennsylvania
1910–1925
Wool, 78 x 78"
Gift of Freyda Rothstein, 1998.8.2

Page 243
Diamond in the Square Quilt
Artist unidentified
Lancaster County, Pennsylvania
1910–1930
Wool, 83⁵⁄₁₆ x 82⁹⁄₁₆"
Gift of Altria Group, Inc., 2008.9.2

Page 244
Sawtooth Diamond in the Square Quilt
Artist unidentified
Lancaster County, Pennsylvania
1921–1935
Wool and rayon, 87 x 85¾"
Gift of Mr. and Mrs. William B. Wigton, 1984.25.3

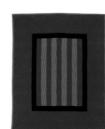

Page 245
Bars Quilt
Artist unidentified
Lancaster County, Pennsylvania
1910–1920
Wool, 87¼ x 72½"
Gift of Mr. and Mrs. William B. Wigton, 1984.25.2

Page 246
Sunshine and Shadow Quilt
Artist unidentified
Lancaster County, Pennsylvania
1930–1940
Wool, rayon, and cotton, 83¾ x 82¾"
Gift of Mr. and Mrs. William B. Wigton, 1984.25.4

Page 247
Double Nine-Patch Quilt
Artist unidentified
Lancaster County, Pennsylvania
1930–1940
Wool and wool-rayon blend, 79½ x 75¾"
Gift of Mr. and Mrs. William B. Wigton, 1984.25.5

Mifflin County Quilts

Page 248
Four in Split Nine-Patch Quilt
Lydia A. (Yoder) Hostetler (dates unknown), embroidered "LAY"
Mifflin County, Pennsylvania, White Topper Amish
1920–1930
Cotton with cotton embroidery, 77 x 67"
Gift of Mr. and Mrs. William B. Wigton, 1984.25.7

Page 249
Four-Patch and Triangles Quilt
Barbara Zook Peachey (1848–1930)
Mifflin County, Pennsylvania, Yellow Topper Amish, Byler Group
1910–1920
Cotton, 85½ x 78¾"
Gift of Mr. and Mrs. William B. Wigton, 1984.25.12

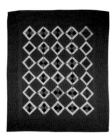

Page 251
Four-Patch in Block-Work Quilt
Annie M. Peachey (Mrs. David M.) Swarey (1902–?)
Mifflin County, Pennsylvania, Yellow Topper Amish, Byler Group
1925–1935
Cotton and rayon, 85 x 72½"
Gift of Mr. and Mrs. William B. Wigton, 1984.25.10

Page 252
Crazy Patch Quilt
Leah Zook Hartzler (dates unknown)
Mifflin County, Pennsylvania, Black Topper Amish, Peachey Group
Dated 1903
Wool and cotton with cotton embroidery, 88 x 75"
Gift of Mr. and Mrs. William B. Wigton, 1984.25.15

Page 253
Log Cabin Quilt, Barn Raising Variation
Lydia A. (Kanagy) Peachey (1863–1949)
Mifflin County, Pennsylvania, Black Topper Amish, Peachey Group
1890–1900
Wool and cotton, 85 x 80½"
Gift of Mr. and Mrs. William B. Wigton, 1984.25.14

Midwestern Quilts

Page 254
Inside Border Child's Quilt
Artist unidentified
Midwestern United States
1925–1935
Cotton, 56 x 44¾"
Gift of George and Carol Henry, 1991.12.1

Page 255
Double Inside Border Quilt
Artist unidentified
Probably Ohio
1910–1925
Cotton, 85½ x 66"
Gift of David Pottinger, 1980.37.55

Page 256
Center Star with Corner Stars Quilt
Unidentified member of the Glick Family
Probably Arthur, Illinois
1890–1900
Wool, 82½ x 76¾"
Gift of Phyllis Haders, 1985.3.1

Page 257
One-Patch Quilt
Artist unidentified
Midwestern United States
Dated 1921
Cotton and wool, 75½ x 64"
Gift of David Pottinger, 1980.37.54

Page 258
Double Nine-Patch Lounge Quilt
Mrs. Dan Troyer (dates unknown)
Holmes County, Ohio
1915–1925
Cotton, 75¾ x 43¼"
Gift of Mr. and Mrs. William B. Wigton, 1984.25.19

Page 259
Pinwheel and Nine-Patch Child's Quilt
Artist unidentified
Midwestern United States
1950–1960
Cotton, 56 x 42"
Gift of Frances Rasmussen in memory of her daughter, Cathyann, 2001.5.3

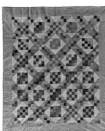

Page 261
Sixteen-Patch Variation Quilt
Artist unidentified
Kalona, Iowa
1950–1960
Cotton, 92 x 86"
Gift of Mr. and Mrs. Alan Weinstein, 2007.15.6

Page 262
Carpenter's Wheel Variation Quilt
Artist unidentified
Midwestern United States
1945–1955
Cotton and synthetics, including nylon, 91 x 81½"
Gift of David Pottinger, 1980.37.41

Page 265
Hummingbirds Quilt
Artist unidentified
Shipshewana, Indiana
1920–1930
Cotton, 87¾ x 68¼" (framed)
Gift of David Pottinger, 1980.37.69

Page 266
Double T Quilt
Artist unidentified
Ohio
1920–1940
Cotton, 82 x 82"
Gift of Frances Rasmussen in memory of her daughter, Cathyann, 2001.5.2

Page 267
Hole in the Barn Door Variation Quilt
Mrs. Menno Yoder (dates unknown), initialed "LMY"
Emma, Indiana
Dated 1942
Cotton, 85 x 74"
Gift of David Pottinger, 1980.37.89

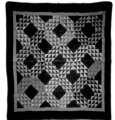

Page 268
Ocean Waves Quilt
Anna Yoder Raber (dates unknown)
Honeyville, Indiana
1925–1935
Cotton and synthetics, 85¾ x 79¾"
Gift of David Pottinger, 1980.37.82

Page 269
Ocean Waves Variation Quilt
Artist unidentified
Emma, Indiana
1920–1930
Cotton, 82½ x 71½"
Gift of David Pottinger, 1980.37.43

Page 270
Tumbling Blocks Quilt
Mrs. Ed Lantz (dates unknown)
Elkhart, Indiana
1910–1920
Cotton, 80½ x 66¼"
Gift of David Pottinger, 1980.37.62

Page 271
Lone Star Quilt
Mrs. David Bontraeger (dates unknown), initialed "DB"
Emma, Indiana
1920–1930
Cotton, 84 x 74" (framed)
Gift of David Pottinger, 1980.37.50

Page 272
Variable Stars Crib Quilt
Artist unidentified
Midwestern United States
1960
Cotton, 44½ x 30"
Gift of Frances Rasmussen in memory of her daughter, Cathyann, 2001.5.1

Page 273
Rolling Stone Quilt
Artist unidentified, initialed "LM"
Indiana
Dated 1925
Cotton, 82¼ x 69"
Gift of David Pottinger, 1980.37.24

Page 274
Double Wedding Ring Quilt
Susie (Mrs. Harry) Bontrager (?–1954)
Yoder, Kansas
1935–1945
Cotton and synthetics, 95½ x 78½"
Gift of Robert Bishop, 1990.25.18

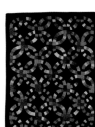

Page 275
Double Wedding Ring Quilt
Mrs. Andy G. Byler (dates unknown)
Atlantic, Pennsylvania
1930–1940
Cotton, wool, linen, and rayon, 84 x 66½"
Gift of Cyril Irwin Nelson in memory of his grandparents Guerdon Stearns and Elinor Irwin (Chase) Holden, and in honor of his parents, Cyril Arthur and Elise Macy Nelson, 1982.22.3

Page 276
Fans Quilt
Artist unidentified, initialed "PM"
Indiana
1925–1935
Cotton, wool, and rayon with cotton embroidery, 82 x 71½"
Gift of David Pottinger, 1980.37.86

Page 277
Chinese Coins Quilt
Sarah Miller (dates unknown)
Haven, Kansas
1935
Cotton, 82⅝ x 62¾"
Gift of David Pottinger, 1980.37.1

Page 278
Sailboats Quilt
Amanda Lehman (dates unknown)
Topeka, Indiana
1955–1965
Cotton, 86¼ x 72"
Gift of David Pottinger, 1980.37.26

Page 279
Trip Around the World Crib Quilt
Artist unidentified
Midwestern United States
1950–1960
Cotton, 37 x 33"
Gift of Frances Rasmussen in memory of her daughter, Cathyann, 2001.5.15

Page 281
Straight Furrow Quilt
Artist unidentified
Kalona, Iowa
1971
Cotton, 92½ x 75¼"
Gift of Mr. and Mrs. Alan Weinstein, 2007.15.8

THE AFRICAN AMERICAN QUILT

Page 284
Strip Quilt
Idabell Bester (?–c. 1992), quilted by Losie Webb (dates unknown)
Alabama
Pieced 1980, quilted 1990
Cotton and synthetics, 83 x 71"
Gift of Helen and Robert Cargo, 1991.19.4

Page 285
Star Quilt
Nora McKeown Ezell (1917–2007)
Eutaw, Alabama
Dated 1977
Cotton and synthetics, 94 x 84"
Museum purchase made possible in part by a grant from the National Endowment for the Arts, with matching funds from the Great American Quilt Festival 3, 1991.13.1

Page 286
Snail Trail Quilt
Mary Maxtion (b. 1924)
Boligee, Alabama
1990
Cotton, 89½ x 77"
Museum purchase made possible in part by a grant from the National Endowment for the Arts, with matching funds from the Great American Quilt Festival 3, 1991.13.2

Page 287
Everybody Quilt
Mary Maxtion (b. 1924)
Boligee, Alabama
1989
Cotton and synthetics, 91½ x 85"
Gift of Helen and Robert Cargo, 1991.19.2

Page 288
Le Moyne Star Variation Quilt
Lucinda Toomer (1888–1983)
Macon, Georgia
1981
Cotton and synthetics, 71¼ x 62"
Gift of Maude and James Wahlman, 1991.32.1

Page 289
Diamond Strip Quilt
Lucinda Toomer (1888–1983)
Macon, Georgia
c. 1975
Cotton corduroy, flannel, velvet, and wool, 79½ x 66¼"
Gift of William Arnett, 1990.7.1

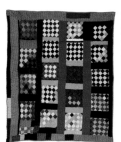

Page 290
Diamond Four-Patch in Cross Quilt
Lureca Outland (c. 1904–2009)
Boligee, Alabama
1991
Cotton and synthetics, 78½ x 83"
Museum purchase made possible in part by a grant from the National Endowment for the Arts, with matching funds from the Great American Quilt Festival 3, 1991.13.6

Page 291
Wedding Ring Interpretation Quilt
Lureca Outland (c. 1904–2009)
Boligee, Alabama
1991
Cotton, wool, and synthetics, 82 x 75"
Museum purchase made possible in part by a grant from the National Endowment for the Arts, with matching funds from the Great American Quilt Festival 3, 1991.13.5

Page 292
Pig Pen Quilt, Log Cabin Variation
Pecolia Warner (1901–1983)
Yazoo City, Mississippi
1982
Cotton, linen, and synthetics, 79½ x 76½"
Gift of Maude and James Wahlman, 1991.32.3

Page 293
Log Cabin Quilt, Courthouse Steps Variation
Plummer T. Pettway (1918–1993)
Boykin, Alabama
1991
Cotton and synthetics, 71½ x 72¾"
Gift of Helen and Robert Cargo, 1991.33.1

Page 302
Polynesia, the Sky
Fran Soika (b. c. 1924)
Novelty, Ohio
Dated 1981
Cotton, 77 x 102"
Gift of Cyril Irwin Nelson in honor of Fran Soika, the artist, 2004.14.4

Page 294
Star of Bethlehem with Satellite Stars Quilt
Leola Pettway (b. 1929)
Boykin, Alabama
1991
Cotton and synthetics, 102 x 93½"
Museum purchase made possible in part by a grant from the National Endowment for the Arts, with matching funds from the Great American Quilt Festival 3, 1991.13.4

Page 304
Reflection
Kathyanne White (b. 1950)
Prescott, Arizona
2001
Hand-dyed cotton, 78 x 48"
Gift of the artist, 2003.11.1

Page 295
Sailboats Quilt
Alean Pearson (b. 1918)
Oxford, Mississippi
1985
Cotton and wool, 88¼ x 80"
Museum purchase made possible in part by a grant from the National Endowment for the Arts, with matching funds from the Great American Quilt Festival 3, 1991.13.8

Page 306
Stars over Hawaii Quilt
Mary K. Borkowski (1916–2008)
Dayton, Ohio
1979
Cotton and polyester with cotton embroidery, 97 x 97"
Gift of Mary K. Borkowski, 1981.5.1

Page 296
Rattlesnake Quilt
Alean Pearson (b. 1918)
Oxford, Mississippi
1985
Cotton and synthetics, 85½ x 80½"
Museum purchase made possible in part by a grant from the National Endowment for the Arts, with matching funds from the Great American Quilt Festival 3, 1991.13.7

Page 307
Bittersweet XII
Nancy Crow (b. 1943), quilted by Velma Brill (dates unknown)
Baltimore, Ohio, and Cambridge, Ohio
1980
Cotton-polyester broadcloth, 79½ x 79"
Gift of Nancy Crow, 1981.3.1

Page 297
Hens Quilt
Pearlie Posey (1894–1984)
Yazoo City, Mississippi
1981
Cotton and synthetics, 71 x 69"
Gift of Maude and James Wahlman, 1991.32.2

Page 308
***Yuen no Akari*: Light from Far-Away Space**
Setsuko Obi (b. 1942)
Tokyo, Japan
2001
Antique Japanese fabrics and hand-woven silk, 78¾ x 48"
Gift of the artist, 2001.30.1

Page 299
Freedom Quilt
Jessie B. Telfair (1913–1986)
Parrott, Georgia
Dated 1983
Cotton with pencil, 74 x 68"
Gift of Judith Alexander in loving memory of her sister, Rebecca Alexander, 2004.9.1

Page 309
Kimono Hanging
Kumiko Sudo (dates unknown)
Berkeley, California
1988
Antique and vintage kimono silks with silk embroidery, 37¾ x 25¾"
Gift of the artist, 1989.11.1

Page 311
Hudson River Quilt
Irene Preston Miller (1917–2007) and the Hudson River Quilters
Croton-on-Hudson, New York
1969–1972
Cotton, wool, and blends with cotton embroidery, 95¼ x 80"
Gift of the J.M. Kaplan Fund, 1991.3.1

Page 313
Untitled Family History Quilt
Hystercine Rankin (b. 1929)
Port Gibson, Mississippi
1990–2000
Fabric with ink, 40 x 62"
Gift of Evelyn S. Meyer, 2005.10.3

Page 315
Kaleidoscopic XVI: More Is More
Paula Nadelstern (b. 1951)
Bronx, New York
Dated 1996
Cottons and silk, 64 x 64"
Gift of the artist, 2008.21.1

Pages 316–317
National Tribute Quilt
Organized and assembled by the Steel Quilters
Pittsburgh
2002
Cotton and mixed media, 8 x 30'
Gift of the artists, Kathy S. Crawford, Amber M. Dalley, Jian X. Li, and Dorothy L. Simback, with the help of countless others in tribute to the victims of the September 11, 2001, attack on America, 2002.14.1

Photographers

Gavin Ashworth, New York: jacket (back), endpapers, and pages 1–5, 8–9, 12–16, 25, 28–32, 34–35, 42–43, 46–47, 54–61, 69–73, 76–83, 86–89, 92, 95–98, 100–102, 111, 114–116, 121, 125–126, 128–129, 132–135, 137–147, 150–151, 159–169, 172–177, 180–184, 187, 190, 196–199, 201, 205, 209–210, 214–215, 219–225, 229, 233, 235–236, 238–239, 242–244, 254, 259–261, 263, 266, 272, 279–281, 288–289, 295, 299, 302–305, 308, 312–313; Karen Bell, New York: page 315; Scott Bowron, New York: pages 53, 112–113, 131, 171, 226, 275, 284–285, 287, 292, 307; Geoffrey Carr, Louisville, Kentucky: pages 230–231; Helga Photo Studio, New York: page 277; Matt Hoebermann, New York: jacket (front) and pages 26, 45, 50, 52, 67, 84–85, 99, 103–107, 127, 191, 194–195, 208, 217, 267–268, 274, 297, 309–311; courtesy In the Beginning Quilts, Inc., Seattle: pages 38–39; Schecter Lee, New York: pages 6–7, 117–119, 148, 156–158, 189, 211–213, 227, 232, 245–248, 251–253, 258, 265; Terry McGinnis, New York: pages 10–11, 63; John Parnell, New York: pages 40–41, 74–75, 110, 124, 185, 271; unidentified: pages 22–23, 27, 33, 36–37, 51, 66, 93, 108–109, 120, 136, 149, 152–153, 186, 192–193, 200, 206–207, 234, 237, 249, 255–257, 262, 269–270, 273, 276, 278, 286, 290–291, 293–294, 296, 306, 316–317.

About the Author

Elizabeth V. Warren is an independent curator, author, collector, and trustee of the American Folk Art Museum, New York. From 1984 to 1991, she was the curator at the museum. Ms. Warren is the coauthor, with Sharon L. Eisenstat, of *Glorious American Quilts: The Quilt Collection of the Museum of American Folk Art* (1996). With Ms. Eisenstat, she also organized a number of exhibitions at the museum, including "Old-Time Favorites, New-Time Fashions: Quilt Revival 1910–1950" (1997), "An American Treasury: Quilts from the Museum of American Folk Art" (1996), and "Victorian Vernacular: The American Show Quilt" (1995). In addition, Ms. Warren served as curator of "Quilts: Masterworks from the American Folk Art Museum" (2010, in conjunction with the present volume), "A Legacy in Quilts: Cyril Irwin Nelson's Final Gifts to the American Folk Art Museum" (2008), "The Perfect Game: America Looks at Baseball" (2003–2004, with catalog), "An Engagement with Folk Art: Cyril I. Nelson's Gifts to the Museum" (2000–2001), "Beyond the Square: Color and Design in Amish Quilts" (1999), "Five-Star Folk Art" (1990, with catalog), and "Young America: A Folk Art History" (1986, with catalog). She received her BA from Bryn Mawr College and her MA in American folk art studies from New York University.

About the Contributors

Maria Ann Conelli is the executive director of the American Folk Art Museum. She was previously dean of the School of Graduate Studies at the Fashion Institute of Technology in New York and, prior to that, chair of the Smithsonian Institution's graduate programs in the History of Decorative Arts in New York and Washington, D.C. Conelli holds a PhD in architectural history from Columbia University and an MA from the Institute of Fine Arts, New York University. She has been the recipient of numerous awards, including the J. Paul Getty Postdoctoral Fellowship in the History of Art and the Humanities, and is a fellow of the American Academy in Rome. Conelli has taught in the United States and in Europe, organized exhibitions, and lectured widely on sixteenth- and seventeenth-century architecture and landscape design.

Martha Stewart is the founder of Martha Stewart Living Omnimedia, Inc., which encompasses award-winning magazines such as *Martha Stewart Living* and *Martha Stewart Weddings*; best-selling books such as *Martha Stewart's Cooking School* and *Martha Stewart's Encyclopedia of Crafts*; the nationally syndicated, Emmy Award–winning daily television series *The Martha Stewart Show*; the marthastewart.com website, featuring the popular Martha Blog; and a broad range of merchandising product lines, including the Martha Stewart Collection of products for the home exclusively at Macy's, Martha Stewart Crafts with EK Success, and more. In 2006, at the American Antiques Show in New York, which is organized annually by the American Folk Art Museum, she was honored with the American Spirit Award for her efforts to create a broad national awareness of Americana and American folk art through her publications and television shows.

Stacy C. Hollander is senior curator and director of exhibitions at the American Folk Art Museum. She has served as curator of numerous exhibitions at the museum, including "Women Only: Folk Art by Female Hands" (2010), "Kaleidoscope Quilts: The Art of Paula Nadelstern" (2009), "The Seduction of Light: Ammi Phillips | Mark Rothko Compositions in Pink, Green, and Red" (2008, with catalog), "Asa Ames: Occupation Sculpturing" (2008), "White on White (and a little gray)" (2006), "Surface Attraction: Painted Furniture from the Collection" (2005), "Blue" (2004), "American Radiance: The Ralph Esmerian Gift to the American Folk Art Museum" (2001, with catalog), and "Harry Lieberman: A Journey of Remembrance" (1991, with catalog); as project coordinator of "Gilded Lions and Jeweled Horses: The Synagogue to the Carousel" (2007, with catalog); and as cocurator, with Brooke Davis Anderson, of "American Anthem: Masterworks from the American Folk Art Museum" (2002, with catalog) and, with Howard P. Fertig, of "Revisiting Ammi Phillips: Fifty Years of American Portraiture" (1994, with catalog). Hollander lectures and publishes widely and is a frequent contributor to scholarly magazines in the field. She received her BA from Barnard College, Columbia University, and her MA in American folk art studies from New York University.